ABOUT THE AUTHOR

Kevin Ruffcorn knows the needs and hopes of growing Christians. He and his wife have grown through their experience with their young son, a cancer patient who responded positively to the care given through medical treatment and through supportive Christian people.

Pastor Ruffcorn has served congregations in North Dakota and Illinois and is now pastor of a church in Oconto Falls, Wisconsin. His book *Sharing the Word* is widely used in personal evangelism.

BIBLE READINGS SERIES

Bible Readings for Women
Lyn Klug
Bible Readings for Men
Steve Swanson
Bible Readings for Parents
Ron and Lyn Klug
Bible Readings for Couples
Margaret and Erling Wold
Bible Readings for Singles
Ruth Stenerson
Bible Readings for Families
Mildred and Luverne Tengbom
Bible Readings for Teenagers
Charles S. Mueller
Bible Readings for Mothers
Mildred Tengbom
Bible Readings for Teachers
Ruth Stenerson
Bible Readings for Students
Ruth Stenerson
Bible Readings for the Retired
Leslie F. Brandt
Bible Readings for Church Workers
Harry N. Huxhold
Bible Readings for Office Workers
Lou Ann Good
Bible Readings for Growing Christians
Kevin E. Ruffcorn
Bible Readings for Caregivers
Betty Groth Syverson
Bible Readings for Troubled Times
Leslie F. Brandt
Bible Readings for Farm Living
Frederick Baltz
Bible Readings on Prayer
Ron Klug
Bible Readings on Hope
Roger C. Palms
Bible Readings on God's Creation
Denise J. Williamson

Bible Readings

FOR GROWING CHRISTIANS

Bible Readings

FOR GROWING CHRISTIANS

Kevin E. Ruffcorn

AUGSBURG Publishing House • Minneapolis

BIBLE READINGS FOR GROWING CHRISTIANS

Copyright © 1984 Augsburg Publishing House

Library of Congress Cataloging in Publication Data

Ruffcorn, Kevin E.
  BIBLE READINGS FOR GROWING CHRISTIANS.

  1. Bible—Meditations.   I. Title.
BS491.5.R84   1984   242'.5   84-18424
ISBN 0-8066-2131-1 (pbk.)

Manufactured in the U.S.A.   APH 10-0685

          4 5 6 7 8 9 0 1 2 3 4 5 6 7 8 9

PREFACE

Someone once remarked, "If we are not busy growing, we are busy dying." Life is constantly changing, and though we would like to "freeze the action," nothing stays the same very long. This is true even of our Christian life.

God is the same yesterday, today, and forever, but we are not. At times our prayers are strong; at other times we cannot even pray. In some situations we have a strong faith; in other situations we doubt. At times we are bold; at other times we are cowards.

God beckons to us to grow in our Christian life. It is not God's will that we remain spiritual babes. We are called to follow God and to grow into strong, mature Christian servants.

The growth God offers to us is *solid* growth, growth that comes from a daily walk with God, study of the Word, and meditation on God's movement in our lives and in our world. It is not a quick growth, nor is it a superficial growth. It is the growth of discipleship.

God also offers to us a *balanced* growth. The Spirit moves in our lives to strengthen our faith, our prayers, our love, and our service. God is not glorified by one who is strong in faith but weak in love. God is glorified by those whose faith is active in love and whose service is backed by prayer.

God has given us the rich gift of life and the ability to grow in that life.

■ THE GIVE AND TAKE OF LIFE

Job 1:13-22:   "The Lord gave and the Lord has
taken away; may the name of the Lord be praised"
(v. 21).

Sally stood by a grave and mourned the loss of her
mother. Ken was excited by a promotion to another
department, but he felt saddened over leaving behind
friends he had worked with for so many years. Dave
was proud of his healthy new son, but he did not like
the loss of his free time. The Hansons were happy
about their daughter's marriage, but they grieved the
loss of their little girl.

We used to feel that grief came to people only at
the death of a loved one. We are now beginning to
realize that grief is a common part of life. We grieve
over whatever we lose. Whether it be the grief of a
young child over the loss of a stuffed animal or an
octogenarian grieving over the loss of youth, grief
comes to everyone.

Life is constantly changing, and with that change
comes loss. God does not keep us from grief or loss.
But in the midst of our loss he gives. God gives us
love, comfort, and strength. God gives us—his children
—faith and hope.

In the midst of our loss we discover that we also
receive. And what we receive is a precious gift from
the Lord, a part of God's abundant life.

 May I praise your name, O Lord, in my loss and
in my gain.

**Write down what you have lost and how you grieve
for it today.**

■ TO GOD BE THE GLORY

1 Cor. 6:12-20: "Therefore honor God with your body" (v. 20).

Ken had worked hard on the Jensen contract. He had attended many meetings and made phone calls to wrap up the loose ends. During the past month he had worked late several nights to make sure that everything was in order. When the contract finally went through, though, it was Ken's boss, the head of the department, who received the credit, the commendation, and a nice bonus.

We have all been in Ken's position at one time or another. We have worked hard, and then someone else has received the credit. We have felt hurt and angry. Imagine how the Lord must feel when we receive the credit which is due to God!

The Lord has called us to be messengers, witnesses, and servants. We are to glorify God in our bodies. The Lord has given us the Spirit to enable us to accomplish our call. When we are successful, we receive praise and honor from those around us.

We can respond to this praise and honor in two ways. We can pass the praise to the Lord, and allow it to bring us to a deeper humility that we have been used to glorify God. Or we can soak up the praise and honor like a sponge and have it fuel our pride and ego. In his book *Markings* Dag Hammarskjöld wrote, "How humble the tool when praised for what the hand has done." How true this is for Christians.

 Lord, forgive me for taking credit for what you have done.

Discuss with another Christian how you give God the glory and how you take the glory away from God.

■ LIVING BY FAITH

2 Cor. 5:6-15:   ''We live by faith, not by sight''
(v. 7).

Tina, the Walkers' first child, was a little over one
year old. Like most one-year-olds Tina was very adept
at traveling around the house. She would latch onto a
piece of furniture and walk around it until she came
to another piece of furniture that she could grab onto.
When confronted by an open area she would go into
"four-wheel drive" and negotiate the space with a
fast crawl. Eventually she would arrive at her
destination.

Like many first-time parents, the Walkers were
anxious for Tina to walk. They would turn her away
from the furniture and stand a few paces away from
her. With outstretched arms they would then say,
"Come to daddy," or "Come to mommy." Tina felt
secure hanging onto a table or a chair. It took her
many weeks to decide to let go and walk to her
parents. At first she took a few tumbles, but soon she
was enjoying her new-found freedom.

We walk through life hanging onto many things.
We hang onto our job, family, house, car, savings
account, and a host of other items. They all give us a
sense of security and peace of mind.

There are times the Lord calls us to let go and
follow. These are difficult times, but when we do let
go, we discover a new freedom.

 Father, help me to let go and follow where
you lead.

List the security items in your life.

■ OBEYING THE RULES

John 15:10-13:   "If you obey my commands, you
will remain in my love, just as I have kept my
Father's commands and remain in his love" (v. 10).

I don't want to be a member of this family any
longer," shouted 18-year-old Jeff. "You're always
telling me what to do and when to do it. You don't
give me any freedom." With that Jeff slammed the
door, drove off in his car, and turned his back on his
family.

Every family has certain rules which its members
live by. These rules vary between families.
Sometimes they are strict, and other times they are
lenient. But in order to enjoy the love, support,
fellowship, and comfort of the family, a person must
follow the rules.

Christians are members of God's family. We are
encouraged to obey the guidance of the Holy Spirit
in our hearts. Yet like Jeff, we struggle. We shun the
guidance of the Holy Spirit and reject any rules as
being too restrictive. We turn our backs on God and
drive off to do what we want.

God's love is not conditional. But God knows that
to partake and enjoy the benefits that come with
membership in his family, we need to obey the
guidance of the Holy Spirit.

 Father, help me to be obedient to your will.

**Recall times when you have excluded yourself from
the benefits of God's family through your lack of
obedience.**

■ ESCAPING TEMPTATION

1 Cor. 10:6-13: "No temptation has seized you except what is common to man. And God is faithful; . . . when you are tempted he will also provide a way out" (v. 13).

Shirley had been deeply hurt by Joan. Joan had spread a rumor about Shirley which was not true. At the church social it was tempting for Shirley to give in to her dislike of Joan and snub her. But she didn't do that. With love and forgiveness she went up to Joan and began to talk to her.

Bob received a bonus in his paycheck. It was tempting to spend that bonus without giving a portion of it to the church. After a struggle within himself Bob first wrote out a check to his church and then went with his family to buy some needed items.

Every day of our lives we are confronted with temptations. Paul writes that with each temptation God provides a way out. That way of escape is no longer the threat of punishment. It has now been changed to the expression of love. God loves us and has given us his Son. Remembering the love of God, we are given the ability to turn from the temptation and walk the path to which Jesus calls.

 Thank you, God, that you do not allow me to be tempted beyond my strength.

Write down some temptations in your life and how you resist them.

■ LOVE IS THE KEY

1 Cor. 13:1-13:   "And now these three remain:
faith, hope, and love. But the greatest of these is
love" (v. 13).

I t was a dark night, and no one had left the outside
house light on. Craig fumbled with his keys, trying to
find the one that fit the door. He tried several before
he found the right one and was able to open it.

Christians struggle to find the key that will open
other people's lives to the gospel of Jesus Christ. Some
say the key is mighty works and miracles that reveal
God's power and glory. Others say it's powerful
preaching that clearly proclaims the gospel. Still
others say it is humanitarian service and working for
peace and justice.

Paul would not disagree with any of these answers.
But he would stress that they all must contain a
common element. They all must be based on love.
For Paul, love was the key that opened people's lives
to the gospel of Jesus Christ.

It was not mighty works or powerful preaching that
drove us into the arms of God. It was God's love
revealed to us in the death and resurrection of
Jesus Christ.

As we share the gospel of Jesus Christ, we do not
need to be talented or special in any way. We only
need to be loving.

 Lord, you love me. Help me to share that love
with others.

**Think of ways in which love has opened the door of
your life.**

16

■ DISPLAYING A TREASURE

2 Cor. 4:5-7: "But we have this treasure in jars of clay to show that this all-surpassing power is from God and not from us" (v. 7).

Brad and Denise entered the jewelry store to look for a diamond engagement ring. They discovered four rings that they liked and asked the jeweler to see them. Each time the jeweler took out a ring for them to look at, he would place it on a piece of velvet. There the diamond would shine in all its brilliance. He did this for a purpose. He did not want anything to detract from the beauty of the diamond.

Christians have a treasure much more beautiful and precious than a diamond. We have the gospel of Jesus Christ. This gospel is on display in our lives.

At times we try so hard to make the display case beautiful. We attempt to be super Christians so that God's power can be more readily apparent to those around us. But we are frustrated in our attempts, and we never escape the everyday setbacks and struggles of life.

God doesn't want super Christians to display his gospel. Their "superness" would detract from the beauty of it. He chooses to display his gospel in the clay jars of our everyday lives. In this way, all the beauty of the gospel is revealed.

 Lord God, thank you for displaying your gospel in my life.

Choose four Christians and think of how the gospel of Jesus Christ is displayed in their everyday lives.

◼ TO KNOW CHRIST

Phil. 3:7-11:   ''I want to know Christ and the power of his resurrection from the dead'' (v. 10).

Russell and Shane grew up together. They were the best of friends, and there was nothing that they did not share with each other. But Shane had to move away, and they were separated by miles. Gradually they knew less and less about each other.

Relationships need to be cultivated in order to grow. They take time, energy, and commitment in order to remain close and healthy. When these elements are not present, the relationship begins to weaken until it is no more.

This same principle is true in our relationship with the Lord. We all desire to know Christ, but that takes time, energy, and commitment. We are challenged to take the time for prayer, Bible study, and meditation. We are encouraged to put forth the energy for worship, praise, and service. We are called to make the commitment to follow where our Lord leads.

Through the death and resurrection of Jesus Christ, we have been given the opportunity of living in a relationship with God. As we live in the reality of that relationship and give the time, effort, and commitment it calls for, the relationship grows. We begin to know Christ and the power of his resurrection.

  Lord Jesus Christ, help me to know you.

Make some changes in your daily life that will help you to spend more time in your relationship with the Lord.

■ THE AROMA OF CHRIST

2 Cor. 2:14-17:   "For we are to God the aroma of Christ among those who are being saved and those who are perishing" (v. 15).

The doorbell rang, and Carol rose to open the door. She discovered a man from a floral company standing on her steps. In his hands he held a bouquet of roses. Excitedly Carol accepted the roses and rushed to put them in a vase and set them in her living room. Soon the room was filled with a lovely fragrance.

Christians compare themselves to many things, but rarely do we see ourselves as fragrant flowers or perfume. Yet that is how Paul described his ministry of proclaiming the gospel. He said he carried the aroma of Christ.

Paul hit the mark with his analogy. All of us have experienced people who walk into a room and give off an aroma of gloom and doom. We have also experienced people who enter a room and bring life and freshness to it.

Christians have a fragrance all our own. Our fragrance is one of hope and love and life. Among the stale odors of everyday life, and in the stench of suffering, pain, and sorrow, it is a welcome fragrance. It is the fragrance of Christ.

 O Christ, may my life be scented with your love, hope, and life.

Imagine yourself entering a room full of people. What impression do you create?

■ SEEKING A SIGN

Matt. 16:1-4: "The Pharisees and Sadducees came to Jesus and tested him by asking him to show them a sign from heaven" (v. 1).

The family knelt in the small hospital chapel. One of their members led them in prayer: "Lord, you are a loving and powerful God. Show us your love and power by answering our prayer and healing Chad."

Fifteen-year-old Chad had been an active boy. On the way home from a ball game, the car in which he was riding was involved in an accident. Chad had received massive internal injuries and was on the critical list.

Chad's life slowly ebbed away. Members of his family continued to pray that God would prove himself and heal Chad. But no miracle happened. Late one night Chad died.

Chad's family was grief-stricken. They were also angry at God. He had not answered their prayers by proving himself a powerful and loving God.

We often believe that God should prove himself to us by answering our prayers. We think God should be able to take away our pain and make life easier.

But God has proven himself another way. God did so many years ago on a cross. There he showed us his love and power.

 Lord God, you are all-powerful and loving. Thank you for showing me this by the cross of Christ.

Read the gospel accounts of Jesus' crucifixion and look for God's love and power.

■ GOD'S KINGDOM IS LIKE YEAST

Matt. 13:31-33:   ''The kingdom of heaven is like
yeast that a woman took and mixed into a large
amount of flour until it worked all through the dough''
(v. 33).

B rad and Brenda watched their mother bake bread.
They stood silently by her side as she poured the
ingredients into the bowl. When their mother mixed
some granules in warm water and then poured it into
the mixture, they became excited. "Mom, what's that?
What's that do?" they asked in unison.

"This is the yeast," their mother replied. "This is
what makes the bread rise and makes it good to eat."

The bread was put on top of the stove to rise, and
the children were sent to the playroom. Every few
minutes they would run into the kitchen to see the
bread dough grow bigger. They were amazed that
the little amount of yeast their mom placed in the
dough could make that much difference.

A little yeast makes a big difference in a lump of
bread dough. The presence of the Lord makes a great
difference in our lives. At times we don't believe we
are growing. But God is like yeast. God grows within
us until all areas of our life are touched.

  Thank you, God, that you are growing within me.

**List ways you have slowly grown and matured in
your Christian life.**

■ THE VINE AND THE BRANCHES

John 15:5-11: "I am the true vine and my Father is the gardener" (v. 5).

The orchard had suffered quite a bit of damage from the windstorm. Tree branches were lying all about on the ground. Young Dave Hayes was helping his father pick up the branches and load them onto the truck. As he did so, he noticed a wet sticky substance on the broken end of the branches. "Hey, dad," he called, "What's this stuff on the end of the branch?"

"That's the tree sap," his father replied. "That's what enables the tree to grow and produce fruit."

What Dave learned was common knowledge, yet the same principle is often forgotten by Christians. We think we need something more in order to lead a fruitful Christian life. So we struggle to get closer to the Lord. We seek some hidden truth that we have overlooked. Or we wallow in guilt because we are not fruitful.

We forget who we are. We are the branches joined to the trunk. The life of the tree is flowing through us. The Holy Spirit moves in and through our lives. The Spirit is the one who produces the fruit.

 Thank you, Jesus, that your life runs through me and bears fruit.

Walk through a garden or orchard. What do you learn about bearing fruit?

■ GOD'S POWER AND AUTHORITY

Luke 7:1-10: "But say the word, and my servant will be healed" (v.7).

P at Coulton put down his morning paper and sipped his coffee. "I don't know what's going on in this world," he said to his wife. "The whole thing seems to be out of control."

"Yes, I know," his wife agreed. "And I don't know why God has let it get this way. The problems in the world seem almost too great for him. I have trouble seeing God answer our prayers about helping Tim with his reading in school, let alone seeing him at work in the Middle East or Central America."

The Coultons face a common question: If God has power and authority, why doesn't God do something? We trip over the word *why*.

No one can answer the question, "Why?" But this does not lead us to despair. We cling to the truth that our God has power and authority. From this truth springs our hope. The God whom we worship is the one who spoke and the world was created. Our God is the one who said the word and the servant was healed.

We cannot answer *why*, but we can proclaim the truth that God does have the power and authority to act.

 Thank you, God, that you are all-powerful.

Pray that God may act with power and authority in your family, in our country, and in the world.

■ GOD'S TRANSFORMING WORK

Rom. 12:1-2: "Do not conform any longer to the pattern of this world, but be transformed by the renewing of your mind" (v. 2).

Cindy took a pottery class. She enjoyed using her hands and special tools to transform a lump of clay into a vessel the size and shape that she wanted.

It dawned on Cindy how the Lord's work in her life was like that of a potter. The Lord was molding her through the power of the Holy Spirit. Through people, events, and the Word, God was transforming her life. She was a different person because of the Lord's activity.

There were many students in Cindy's class. Each molded their clay into a different form, to be used for a different purpose. The Lord is not the only potter. The world also seeks to mold Christians. It works to conform us to its shape and its standard.

The shape our life takes depends on which potter's wheel we are on. Paul appeals to us to place ourselves on the wheel of the Lord and be transformed by God's work in our lives.

 Lord, have your own way in my life. You are the potter and I am the clay.

Divide a sheet of paper in half. On one side list how you are conformed to the world. On the other side list how God has transformed your life.

24

■ GOD KNOWS OUR NEEDS

Ps. 139:1-6:   "You know when I sit and when I
rise; you perceive my thoughts from afar" (v. 2).

At birthdays and Christmas Bob and Jane would
open the gifts from their grandmother first. She always
knew just what they needed, and her gifts were
always the right size and color.

Their grandmother did not have an uncanny power
which enabled her to do this. She lived close to Bob
and Jane, and she visited with them often.

When Bob and Jane moved away with their family,
they saw their grandmother only once a year. Before
birthdays and Christmas their grandmother would
call and ask them what they wanted and what sizes
they wore. Even then the gifts she gave often needed
to be returned. They were the wrong size, color,
or style.

The God we worship lives with us and is intimately
involved in our lives. God knows our needs and
sometimes meets those needs even before we ask.
God's gifts to us are abundant, yet "tailor-made."

There is much comfort in knowing that God is close
and cares.

 Thank you, Father, that you know me and that
you are meeting my needs.

**Make a list of gifts you have received from God that
were just what you needed.**

■ PROVIDING FOR OUR NEEDS

Matt. 6:25-33:   ''Therefore I tell you, do not worry about your life, what you will eat or drink'' (v. 25).

Matt was an engineer at a manufacturing company. He had a good job and took home a good salary. Matt was proud of the fact that he could work hard and provide so well for his family.

Suddenly Matt suffered a stroke. He was in the hospital for only three weeks, but it was almost a year before he recovered and was able to return to work. During that time Matt's salary was gone, and he and his family had only disability insurance and savings to see them through. Times were tough, but the family drew on their faith and believed that God would provide for their needs.

Matt and his family are like many Christians. They see God working in their lives only when times are tough. But this is not the message of Scripture. We are like the birds of the air and the flowers of the field, whose Creator is at all times touching them and moving among them. Yes, we work hard, but it is God who daily provides for our needs.

 Lord, forgive me when I take credit for something you have done.

Write down how God has provided for you this past week. Then spend some time giving thanks.

■ GOD IS OUR CASTLE

Ps. 27:1-3:   "The Lord is the stronghold of my life—
of whom shall I be afraid?" (v. 1).

T he hill rose above the lush green German forest.
On its crown a castle had been built with high, thick
walls. It was an impenetrable fortress. It had survived
many attacks, and from it many attacks had been
launched.

What a comforting thought it is to know that the
Lord is our castle, our stronghold. We need Christ in
that way. When the activities of our daily lives drain
us of our energy, we run to our castle for rest.
Sometimes the world turns hostile, and we stand
behind the castle's thick walls for protection.

But a castle was not used only for defensive
purposes. From it attacks were launched. Within the
castle people would be nourished and strengthened.
They would organize for the attack and go forward as
a strong army.

God is our protection from the world, but we are
not separated from the rigors of life. God is our
castle where we go to be nourished and strengthened
for our primary mission: to proclaim the good news of
Jesus Christ.

Thank you, God, that you are my castle.
Strengthen me that I may boldly proclaim your
gospel.

**Divide a piece of paper in half. On one side list the
ways God shields you. On the other half list how
God enables you to share the good news.**

■ GOD'S PRUNING

John 15:1-5: "Every branch that does bear fruit
he trims clean so that it will be even more fruitful"
(v. 2).

A small bush grows in front of my house. In order
for it to be the right size and shape it needs to be
pruned. I take a snip here and another snip there,
and soon the bush is just the way I want it to be.

What a surprise it was for me to see how
vinedressers prune grapevines. They don't snip off a
few long branches in order that a vine might look
nice. They prune the vine back to the main stem and
sometimes right down to the ground. The vinedresser
is not concerned about looks; they want the vine to
produce.

We Christians want the Lord to prune us with a few
snips. We want our lives to be cleaned up. We want a
Christian life with substance that others will praise
God for.

But the Lord doesn't stop with a mere snip. Christ
cuts deep into our lives, severing our fears, our
prejudices, our selfishness, and our pride. By the time
he is finished, only a stump remains, the stump of his
never-failing grace and love in our lives.

The Lord's pruning may hurt at times, but from it
our lives grow with a lushness that bears much fruit.

 Thank you, Lord, for pruning my life so that I
may bear fruit for you.

**List areas where you have been pruned and how you
are now bearing fruit because of it.**

■ NOTHING CAN SEPARATE US FROM GOD

Rom. 8:31-39: ". . . nor anything . . . in all creation, will be able to separate us from the love of God that is in Christ Jesus our Lord" (v. 39).

Steve drove past the crowded church parking lot. "I can't go back," he thought to himself. "I've made a mess of things. If I can't forgive myself, God can't either."

Sarah stared at her husband's picture. It had been four weeks since his sudden death. She felt God had turned his back on her. In her loneliness she did not feel God's presence.

The Wilsons stood holding each other and watched the firemen put out the fire in their home. "Where is God, if he allows something like this to happen?" they wondered.

The apostle Paul had been through it all. He had been beaten for his faith and shipwrecked. He had known hunger and thirst and want. In this he had discovered what he wrote to the Romans: that nothing could separate believers from God.

This is true today. Sin doesn't separate us from God, because God still reaches out to us in forgiveness. Death doesn't separate us, for God comes to us in hope and comfort. Tragedy doesn't separate us, because God continues to provide for us. In all of life God is with us.

 Thank you, God, for your continuing presence in my life.

Remember a time you felt God had left you. When did you realize once again that God is always by your side?

■ CARRYING EACH OTHER'S BURDENS

Gal. 6:1-5: "Carry each other's burdens, and in this way you will fulfill the law of Christ" (v. 2).

The cries for help split the cold night air. Lights flashed on in homes as people inside heard the screams. But no one came to help. No one even called the police. They did nothing, because no one wanted to get involved.

The car was stalled on a well-traveled stretch of road. It was obvious that there was car trouble. Yet the driver could not get anyone to stop. No one wanted to get involved.

The way of the world is not to get involved. It's too risky, and it may involve too much time and effort. So people ignore the cries for help until they become their own cries.

Christ calls us to get involved and to bear each other's burdens. The love and the talents that he has given us are to be used to help others. To answer God's call involves effort, time, and sacrifice. But it is our call.

God gives us gifts and encourages us to spend them freely on others.

 Father, help me to use my gifts to serve others.

Someone is in need today. Take the time and make the effort to carry their burden.

◼ TIMES OF DESPAIR

2 Cor. 4:7-12: "We are hard pressed on every side, but not crushed; perplexed, but not in despair" (v. 8).

Pilgrim in his travel to the Celestial City in *Pilgrim's Progress* encountered the Slough of Despond. When Pilgrim encountered the Slough, his feet began to get stuck in the mud, and he began to sink.

This is a poignant description of despair. No matter where we are in our Christian lives, we all encounter the swamp. When we do, we slow down. Our feet become too heavy to lift, because they are caked with the mud of doubt and worry. We begin to sink in the swamp, and we fear we might be in over our head.

In his second letter to the Corinthians Paul stated that he had been perplexed, but not in despair. What did he do to keep from getting stuck in the swamp? The answer lies in the words, "We have this treasure in jars of clay, to show that this all-surpassing power is from God." Paul's victory over despair was through the power of God.

When people get stuck in the swamp they cannot free themselves. The more they struggle the more they sink. When we encounter despair in our lives, our only hope is to reach out to our God. God is the one who can pull us out and set us on the path once again.

 O Lord, pull me out of my despair.

Write down a time you despaired and describe how God may have been working in your life.

■ DISAPPOINTMENT

Ps. 42:1-5:   "Why are you downcast, O my soul?
Why so disturbed within me?" (v. 5).

Jill was disappointed as she left her supervisor's
office. She had been expecting a raise in pay.
Now it would not be coming. All salaries were frozen
at her company. Gone were all those wonderful
dreams.

Don was disappointed as he walked out of his
classroom and headed toward his car. The class just
wasn't going right. The kids didn't seem to be
learning the material.

Life is full of disappointments. These disappointments often come when our own wills are not
done. We have things figured out, and we know
how they should go. When they do not go that way,
we feel disappointed.

The psalm writer felt the same way. God was not
playing by the psalmist's game plan. Things were not
going the way he wanted them to, and he was facing
some hard times.

But in the midst of disappointment the psalm writer
gave us the key to rise above it: "Put your hope in
God, for I will yet praise him, my Savior and my
God." The solution for disappointment is not always
to get our way. The solution is to place our hope in
God and to have the faith that God's will is being
done in our lives.

 O Savior, in my disappointment, may your will
and not mine be done.

**List disappointments which turned out to be
diamonds.**

■ USING OUR TALENTS

Matt. 25:14-30: "Well done, good and faithful servants! You have been faithful with a few things; I will put you in charge of many things" (v. 21).

Carrie attended worship services regularly. She enjoyed singing the hymns, listening to the sermon, and being with other members of the congregation.

At times Carrie would be asked to get more involved in the congregation. She was once asked to help organize a craft show; another time, to help on the worship committee. Both times she said no. It was not that Carrie did not want to get involved in her church; she honestly felt she had no abilities to serve with.

Jesus' parable of the talents underlines a truth we see everyday in our lives: some people have more abilities than others. But it also points out that everyone has some ability. Even the unworthy servant started out with two talents.

Some Christians bemoan the fact that they are not as gifted as others. They waste much time wishing they had more ability. This is not what we are about.

Each of us has abilities. We are challenged to discover these and then to use them to serve God.

 Lord, you have given me many talents. Help me use them in service to you.

What is one of your abilities? How are you using it to serve God?

■ REPENTANCE

Ps. 51:10-12:   "Create in me a pure heart, O God,
and renew a steadfast spirit within me" (v. 10).

Dennis and Sue were on their way to a party in a
subdivision on the other side of the city. It was an
area they had not been in before.

As they traveled, Sue called out the turns to Dennis.
Even though they thought they followed the
directions closely, they took a wrong turn. They began
to pass by farms rather than subdivisions. They had to
turn around and go another direction.

King David was much like Dennis and Sue. He
too took a wrong turn: he committed murder and
adultery. When God confronted him with his sin,
David repented—turned around and again walked the
right path.

We too make wrong turns and sin. Sometimes we
misread the directions. At other times we reject God's
guidance and follow another path that interests us.
Whatever the case, we need to turn around.

That turning around is *repentance*. God confronts
us by the Holy Spirit. The Spirit points out to us that
we have taken the wrong path and leads us back to
the path God wants us to walk.

 I walk many wrong paths, O God. Enable me to
repent and to walk only your path.

**Remember a time you turned around from a path you
were following in order to follow God's path.**

■ HABITS THAT TARNISH

Rom. 7:13-20: "I do not understand what I do. For what I want to do I do not do, but what I hate, I do" (v. 15).

D an walked through the plant without saying a word to most of the people he met. He had a habit of ignoring people. Unless he asked them to do something, he wouldn't acknowledge their presence. This hurt many people.

When confronted with his behavior by concerned friends, he did not feel he could change. His excuse was, "It's just a habit."

Experts estimate that almost two-thirds of our actions are done out of habit. Some habits are good, some habits are bad. All habits can be changed.

We have heard, "Actions speak louder than words," even actions done out of habit. To reflect the glory of God, Christians need to change bad habits into good ones.

Habits are changed first by confessing them and asking the Lord to help us change. Secondly, we concentrate on replacing our bad habit with a good habit. Dan could concentrate on talking to people as he walked.

It takes effort to change a bad habit into a good one. But then it takes effort to be a disciple of Jesus Christ.

 Lord, I want you to be glorified in all of my life, including my habits.

Decide which habit you'd like to change. Then concentrate on replacing that habit with a good one for the next month.

■ CONFESSION OF SIN

1 John 1:5-10: "If we confess our sins, he is faithful and just and will forgive us our sins" (v. 9).

Someone must have nicked me in the parking lot," Kyle said as he sat down to supper. "There's a scratch on the left front fender. I hope I can cover it up with some paint."

A few hours after supper one of Kyle's sons came to him and wanted to talk. "Dad," he said, "the car didn't get scratched in the parking lot. I scratched it two days ago when I was putting my bike in the garage. I didn't tell you, because I was afraid you'd be angry."

"I'm glad you came and talked to me," said Kyle. "I'm more proud that you confessed than I am angry at what you have done. Why don't you plan on helping me paint over that scratch this Saturday."

Jesus died on the cross so that the sins of all humankind might be forgiven. Though our sins are forgiven, we still need to confess them.

We confess our sins because the burden of sin and guilt is heavy to bear. It is lifted only by confession. We also confess our sins in order to be told once again that we are forgiven and that we are loved.

 Lord, I have sinned. Forgive me!

Remember a time when you needed to confess something in order to "get it off your chest."

■ JEALOUSY

Gal. 5:15-21: "The acts of the sinful nature are obvious: . . . jealousy" (vv. 19-20).

The parents faced a dilemma. Timmy needed snow-pants, and Todd needed gloves. The dilemma was that their budget would not allow them to buy both children their clothes at the same time. They decided to purchase the gloves for Todd. The snow pants would come out of the next paycheck.

The next evening Todd received his gloves after supper. Timmy was downcast. "Don't I get anything?" he asked.

"Not right now," replied his father. "You'll get your snowpants in two weeks."

That wasn't enough for Timmy; he wanted his snowpants now. He left the table crying and went up to his room.

His father went up, took Timmy in his arms, and said, "We love you, Tim. We love you as much as we do Todd. Even if we could give you many things, we wouldn't be able to love you any more." The words weren't as consoling as a new pair of snowpants, but Timmy was soon off playing.

How often we act like Timmy when others are blessed by God. Yet all we need to do is to look to the cross to know that we are loved.

 Father, forgive me for my jealousy. Thank you for your love.

In what areas are you jealous of others? Why?

■ FRESH GRACE

Lam. 3:19-26: "His compassions never fail. They are new every morning" (vv. 22-23).

The fresh-cut flowers sitting on the dining room table brightened the room and freshened the air with their fragrance. Within a few days, though, they began to wilt and lose their color. The water they were in turned green. The flowers needed to be replaced with fresher ones.

There are times when our relationship wth God begins to wilt. This is not because God has turned his back on us. Usually we have neglected the relationship. We have turned our back on God and taken our life together for granted. When we do not look to God today, we begin to live in the past and talk about what God *has done* rather than what God *is doing*.

Life with God can be fresh. It can be experienced every day, because God's love and mercy are new every day.

 Thank you Father, that I can walk with you today and experience your love in a fresh way.

List the ways in which God has acted in your life today.

■ GOD IS OUR HELP

Psalm 121: "My help comes from the Lord, the Maker of heaven and earth" (v. 2).

Sally reminisced about her childhood. She could still remember her first sewing project. She stood in front of a table full of cloth saying, "I can't do it, mom. I just can't do it."

Sally's mom put her arm around the girl and said, "Yes, you can." Sally was about to say she couldn't when her mom repeated, "Yes, you can, because I will help you."

Now Sally was a big girl and on her own. Mom was hundreds of miles away in another city. Who was going to help her? She was having trouble at work with an employee who did not work well with the other employees. The competition had been fierce, and her spirits had been worn down this past year. She was tired and didn't think she could continue. But to whom could she look for help?

In her dilemma Sally sat down and paged through the Bible. Her eyes fell on this verse, "My help comes from the Lord." Yes, God is our help, not only in our distress, but every day of our lives.

 Lord, teach me to look to you for help.

Remember how God helped you in a situation in which you were having trouble.

■ GOD IS NUMBER ONE

Luke 9:59-60: "Jesus said to him: 'Let the dead bury their own dead, but you go and proclaim the kingdom of God' " (v. 60).

After a tearful good-bye, Frank and Ellen boarded a plane to fly to their new home. They had felt the call to become overseas missionaries. It had not been an easy decision. Yet they knew they must follow their call; their service to God came first.

The housewife who decides to seek work outside the home faces a decision similar to that of Frank and Ellen. So does the executive who ponders a career change, and the retired couple with newfound leisure time. All must decide how best to serve God.

Decisions are made after considering many factors. We look at income, career advancement, family, and job satisfaction—to name a few. These are important considerations, yet they are not the primary factor.

For the Christian the primary factor in decision making is "What is God calling me to? How can I best serve God?" This is primary because God is number one in our lives.

 Lord, guide me that I may serve you.

What factors do you consider in making your decisions?

■ THE POWER OF OUR WORDS

James 1:26; 3:3-6:   "If anyone considers himself religious and yet does not keep a tight rein on his tongue, he deceives himself and his religion is worthless" (v. 26).

The district manager stuck his head into Ken's office and said, "I really liked how you handled the Adams account, Ken. Keep up the good work." Those words made Ken's day.

Karen was looking for a client's file. "I put it right next to the copy machine," she muttered. "That was a stupid thing to do," her supervisor responded. "You knew it would get lost." The words hurt Karen and spoiled her day.

In schoolyards children chant the rhyme, "Sticks and stones will break my bones, but words will never hurt me." Perhaps we would like to believe it's true, but it's not.

Words have great power. Because of this Christians' tongues need the lordship of Jesus as much as their hearts do.

We are not called to put away all criticism and to speak only empty words of praise. We are called to put away unkindness and to speak only words of love. Words of love, whatever form they take, bring life.

 Loving God, may my words be filled with love and life.

Speak words of love today to those around you and notice the change that the words make.

■ A SPRING FOR DRY TIMES

John 4:7-15: "The water I give him will become in him a spring of water welling up to eternal life" (v. 14).

It was a time of struggle for Don and Cindy. A major change at Don's work had placed him under a boss he did not like to work for. At Cindy's shop production had been cut back, and Cindy found herself working only half days.

Don and Cindy were also having trouble with their children. Sue, a fifth grader, was having trouble in reading and needed special tutoring. They suspected that D. J., their 14-year-old, was using drugs.

Don and Cindy's world was coming apart. They felt drained of life. In the midst of their troubles they looked to God. Together they prayed and asked God for help. They read the Scriptures, and in them they found comfort and strength.

God did not take away the problems that Don and Cindy faced. But he did become a spring of water for them in their dry times.

 O Holy Spirit, I thank you for being a spring of water in my life.

Take time today to drink deeply from God's spring.

■ SOMETIMES I'M AFRAID

1 John 4:17-21:   "There is no fear in love. But perfect love casts out fear" (v. 18).

Mom, dad," came the small voice from the upstairs bedroom, "I'm scared!"

"Go to sleep, Paul. There's nothing to be scared of!" came the reply from the living room.

A few minutes later sounds of crying were heard. Moved with compassion and a bit of irritation, the father climbed the stairs. Sitting on the bed, he took Paul in his arms and listened as Paul told of creatures in his room.

The father searched the room for the creatures. After a hug and a kiss Paul settled into a sound sleep. His fears had been taken away by love.

Fear is part of a Christian's life. It doesn't come from lack of faith, but from walking on a new path. It doesn't go away when we tell ourselves we have nothing to fear. It flees when we see the love of God in our lives.

 Father, so often I'm scared. Help me remember your love.

This week when you find you are scared, remind yourself of God's love for you.

■ SLOW GROWTH

Col. 2:1-7: ". . . rooted and built up in him, strengthened in the faith as you were taught" (v. 7).

The subdivision was about 30 years old, built on a stretch of prairie with no trees. When the people moved into their homes, they immediately planted trees.

Most of the residents wanted shade quickly. They planted fast-growing trees like Chinese elm and cottonwood. Some of the residents wanted trees they thought were beautiful and would last. They planted oak and hard maple.

Now 30 years later, it is the oak and maple trees that have survived. The others died long ago.

In our Christian life we all wish we could grow more quickly. We get upset with ourselves at our actions that do not bring glory to God. And we kick ourselves when we fall back into old habits that we thought we had discarded long ago.

At these times it is good to remember that we are like oaks and maples. Rooted and built up in Christ, our growth is slow but sure.

 Lord Jesus may I grow strong in your Word.

Look at a tree and meditate on how it has grown.

■ PRAISING OTHERS

Col. 1:3-8: "We always thank God, the Father of our Lord Jesus Christ, when we pray for you" (v. 3).

W hen Shirley arrived at her desk, she found a note directing her to see her boss. She walked over to his office with questions of *why?* running through her head. She timidly knocked on the door.

"Oh, Shirley, come on in," he said. "I just wanted to tell you how pleased I was with your work on the Johnson contract. You did a very good job. Keep up the good work."

Encouraged by that word of praise, Shirley worked hard to do even better.

We all respond to praise. But few of us give praise to others. Praise is one of the simplest acts of love—and also one of the most welcome. Praise is one way we encourage each other in the faith.

Paul must have known this. In most of his letters he started out with a word of praise to the people of the church. We are challenged by his example.

 Open my eyes, Lord, that I might see occasions for praise. Then help me to give that praise.

Every day give someone an honest word of praise.

■ THE CROSS AND THE CHRISTIAN

Mark 8:34-38: ''If anyone would come after me, he must deny himself and take up his cross and follow me'' (v. 34).

Kathy opened the wrapped box and discovered a silver cross. "Oh, it's beautiful! I'll wear it wherever I go!" she exclaimed.

How different this scene is from the words of Jesus. The disciples must have been horrified when they thought of the implications of what he said. The cross was a symbol of suffering. It was the means of a cruel and dishonorable death. After Jesus' death and resurrection the cross came to mean total self-denial.

We bear the cross when we deny ourselves. That may mean that we alter our life-style so that we are able to give more to alleviate world hunger. It may mean that we have less leisure time because we are expressing our faith through a service project. There are many possibilities.

We bear the cross and deny ourselves because we follow one who bore the cross for us.

 Lord Jesus, help me to bear the cross for you.

In what ways are you a crossbearer?

■ OUR WEAKNESS IS GOD'S STRENGTH

2 Cor. 12:7-10: "My grace is sufficient for you, for my power is made perfect in weakness" (v. 9).

It was a long hike, and young Chris's legs were beginning to give out on him. He and his family had been hiking since early morning. Now he sat down on a rock in the noon heat and called out, "Dad, I just can't walk another step."

"That's OK," he said. "I can carry you on my back for a little while. We don't have too far to go to get back to the car anyway."

There are many times in our lives when we feel like Chris. We have traveled a long distance, and the path of service we have been called to or the situation we have gotten ourselves into has sapped all our strength. We feel that we cannot go a step farther.

At times like these our heavenly Father stoops down and picks us up. *We* may not be able to go the distance, but *he* is. In the time of our weakness he is our strength.

 Thank you, Father, for giving me strength for today.

When you are faced with a difficult task today, look to God for the strength to accomplish it.

■ FAITH AND WORKS

James 2:18-26: "Show me your faith without deeds, and I will show you my faith by what I do" (v. 18).

The Mailers went on a vacation to Florida last year. They had a great time lying in the sun and absorbing its warmth. They sat back with no schedule to harass them.

Odd as it may seem, many people use the church in the same way the Mailers used their vacation. They attend a worship service and bask in the grace and mercy of the Lord. They sing hymns and celebrate all that the Lord has done for them. Then they sit back and enjoy being a Christian.

They don't like the idea of works and feel it is contrary to grace. But they have forgotten something: when God saved us by grace, God freed us to a life of service. That life of service involves both grace and works.

When the Mailers returned from their Florida vacation, they were rested and ready to enter into their busy life-style once again. When we leave our worship, we have been prepared for service.

 Lord, help me to work for you today.

In thankfulness for what God has done, be of service to someone today.

◼ TEMPTATION FOR GLORY

Phil. 2:3-6: "Your attitude should be the same as that of Christ Jesus: Who, being in very nature God, did not consider equality with God something to be grasped" (vv. 5-6).

S tan mounted the stage to receive his prize. It had taken a lot of training and discipline, but he had finally accomplished his goal of winning a marathon.

Stan is one of those fortunate people who wins the prize in many areas of life. He is successful in his business. He has a wonderful marriage, and he is very active in his church.

Many people in Stan's church also wanted to give him a prize. He had headed up a stewardship drive that put the church well over the top of their budget. Instead they gave him power and authority in the church.

Stan was at the top of the church, just as he was in the other areas of his life. Then he read this passage of Scripture. Jesus, who was at the very top, turned from the glory and climbed down in order that he might serve.

That passage of Scripture changed Stan's life, as it can ours.

 O God, help me to climb down from my glory mountain so that I may serve others.

List areas in which you are too proud to serve.

■ MAKING DIFFICULT DECISIONS

Judges 6:36-40:   ''Then I will know that you will
save Israel by my hand, as you said'' (v. 37).

Gideon had a hard decision to make. He had to
determine if it was the right time to lead an army
against the Midianites and deliver Israel from their
rule. He wanted to make sure he was following God's
will. So he laid out a fleece.

John was faced with a difficult decision. He had
been approached by another company and offered a
job. It would be an advancement with a salary
increase. But it would entail moving to a different
city far from friends and family. John wanted to
make the right decision, and he wanted to do God's
will.

Today Christians are faced with difficult decisions.
There are many paths to follow, and often we do
not know which one to take. We want to do the Lord's
will, but do not always know what that will is.

The story of Gideon and the fleece encourages
us to seek God's guidance. God does lead us and
make his will known—through other people, through
his Word, through circumstances, and through our
own thoughts. When we ask for God's guidance and
help in making decisions, God will answer our prayer.

 O Spirit of wisdom, make your will known to me.

**Take time to seek God's will for the difficult
decisions you will make this week.**

■ LEARNING TO FORGIVE

Matt. 18:21-35: "I tell you, not seven times, but seventy-seven times" (v. 22).

J eff slammed the door and stormed through the house. A friend had let him down by not helping as he had promised. The friend's negligence had caused the near disaster of a program.

Jeff was angry because he had been wronged. He wanted to strike back at his friend because he had been hurt.

While Jeff was storming around the house, his wife came up to him and asked him if he had picked up the craft items she needed for her banner committee. Jeff had completely forgotten, and now it was too late to pick up anything. The committee would be unable to finish the banner as they had wanted to.

"That's all right, honey," his wife said. "We all forget things. I forgive you."

Suddenly all of Jeff's anger at his friend's negligence was gone. They had both made mistakes. Jeff had been forgiven for his and was now challenged to forgive his friend.

It is easy to forget that we are in need of forgiveness—from others and from God. When we do forget, we feel people have done things that deserve our anger. The truth Christ offers is that they have done things that deserve our forgiveness.

 Father, you have forgiven me and so have many others. Help me also to forgive.

Think of a person whom you have not forgiven and find a way to express your forgiveness.

■ BEING STRONG IN THE LORD

Eph. 6:10-17:   "Finally, be strong in the Lord and in his mighty power" (v. 10).

Tim was one of the smaller kids in his class and the target of the school bullies. He was always coming home with a bloody nose and torn shirt. Finally Tim was afraid to go to school.

Then Tim discovered a secret weapon—his older brother. When he was by Tim's side, the school bullies left Tim alone. Once again Tim had the courage to go to school.

We too discover that life throws some hard punches. Our eyes get blackened and our noses get bloodied and we begin to view life as an ordeal to go through. We cringe at the thought of becoming more involved through Christian service.

But the Lord is by our side. Christ gives us the strength to face the rigors of life. Like our big brother, Jesus joins our fights. He fends off some of the blows, and he nurses our wounds when we are hurt.

As Christ walks by our side, God's strength becomes our strength. It is a gift to enable us to live abundantly and to God's glory.

 Thank you for the strength you give me to face each new day, O Lord. Help me to be strong in you.

Write down how the Lord has given you strength during the past week.

■ DEALING WITH DOUBTS

Mark 9:20-24:   "Immediately the boy's father
exclaimed, 'I do believe; help me overcome my
unbelief!' " (v. 24).

If you doubt, then you don't really have faith," the
friend said. That cast Bob into a tailspin. He always
had a little doubt mixed in with his faith.

When his church voted for a building program, he
believed they could afford it; but there still was
doubt. When his wife was pregnant, he prayed for
a healthy baby; but there still was doubt.

Bob's struggle is that of every Christian. We find
ourselves echoing the cry of the father, "Lord, I do
believe. Help me overcome my unbelief." This is not
the cry of the faithless. It is the cry of a person who
is walking a new path or setting off on a new
adventure with the Lord.

There are times, though, when doubts are so
strong they almost swallow up our faith. There are
many things we can do to fight off those doubts. The
first one is to do exactly as the father did: he confessed
his doubts and asked for help. Another idea is to
remember the ways the Lord has moved in our lives
in the past. We can also meditate on God's promises
of love and concern for us.

Doubt is a part of the Christian life; it never goes
away completely. But when we look on our Lord
and see Christ's love, concern, and power, our doubts
fade.

 Lord, I struggle in my faith with doubts. Help
me in my struggle.

**Take time to list the doubts that are troubling you.
Then confess them to the Lord and ask for his help.**

■ HUNGER FOR GROWTH

Matt. 5:1-12:   "Blessed are the meek, for they will inherit the earth" (v. 5).

Jim ran the verse, "Blessed are those who hunger . . ." through his mind as he looked at the poster of the starving child. He thought, "If that's what hunger is, why is it blessed?"

On his way home from the church service, Jim had a sudden craving for a hamburger and fries. Unable to get the craving out of his mind, he turned to his family and said, "Let's go and eat at a restaurant today."

Most well-fed Americans have had no experience with hunger, but all of us know what it is to have a craving. Whether it be for a piece of fruit, a malt, or a candy bar, we have all been driven.

When Jesus talks about hungering after righteousness, he is talking about a craving. A Christian is to have a driving desire to live a life that is pleasing to God and one which gives God glory. This is the hunger that is called *blessed*, and that is followed by a promise of being filled.

This craving comes from deep within us. It is one of God's gifts to us, a precious gift that opens the road to a growing Christian life.

 O Holy Spirit, work in my life and give me a craving for righteousness and a desire for a deeper walk with you.

List areas of your life where you need to grow.

54

■ CALLED TO BE HOLY

1 Cor. 1:1-3: ''To the church of God in Corinth, to those sanctified in Christ Jesus and called to be holy'' (v. 2).

M oses saw a burning bush and was called to lead the people of Israel to the promised land. David, while tending his flock, received a message to come home and was annointed king of Israel. Paul, riding off to Damascus, was struck from his horse and became an apostle to the Gentiles.

All these people were called by God. In Paul's greeting to the church at Corinth we are reminded that this calling is not reserved only for the greats of the Bible. God calls each one of us into a relationship and a life of service.

We are probably not called to be a father of a nation. Perhaps we are not even called to be great Christian leaders. But we are called to be God's saints, God's holy ones. We are called to be messengers where we work. We are called to be God's teachers and examples in our families. We are called to be servants in our church and in the community in which we live.

Though the places and times may be different, God has called every Christian to be holy. It is an important call that ought not be taken lightly.

 Father, thank you for calling me into a life of service and a relationship with you. Help me to be your saint, your holy one in all areas of my life.

List ways you are God's holy one in your daily life.

■ GROWTH THROUGH STRUGGLE

James 1:2-4: "Consider it pure joy, my brothers, whenever you face trials of many kinds, because you know that the testing of your faith develops perseverance" (v. 2).

Ted was sitting at his desk when he began to feel a sharp pain above his temple. Then in one quick motion he toppled to the floor. That was the last thing Ted remembered until he awoke in the hospital emergency room. Ted had had a stroke.

Lying in bed, Ted became angry. He continually asked himself, "Why me?" He was also a little jealous of those people who were healthy. When he looked at the struggle toward recovery and a healthy lifestyle, Ted became depressed.

No one likes to struggle in life. We often become angry over it, and occasionally a bit depressed. We see it as an interruption and an inconvenience in our everyday lives. But God sees it as a classroom.

Much can be learned through the study of Scripture, the reading of books, and the discussion of personal beliefs. But all of this takes on a new meaning in our lives in the midst of struggle. Then we begin to see the true meaning of forgiveness and the necessity of grace. In struggle we see how weak we are and how strong God is. It is the furnace God uses to mold us into the image of Christ.

 Thank you for the struggles in my life, Father, and for helping me to grow through them.

Recall how God has touched your life through struggles.

■ GOD—THE GIVER OF GROWTH

1 Cor. 3:5-9: "I planted the seed, Apollos watered it, but God made it grow" (v. 6).

Diane received the houseplant from a friend when she moved into her new apartment. She was careful to place it in a spot where it would get enough sun, and she was cautious not to over-water it. With Diane's care, the plant thrived and began to grow.

In his letter to the Corinthians Paul compared the Christian's life to a plant. That life is planted, it is watered, and it grows. But look at who is responsible for the growth—God! It was not Paul the planter or Apollos the caretaker who gave the growth. It was God.

We can take care of the life within us as Diane did her houseplant. We can make sure that we get plenty of light by exposing ourselves to God's Word. The water comes from worship, fellowship, and service. We *encourage* growth by these activities, but we do not *produce* it. Our growth is a gift from God.

Our life with God came to us as a gift. When we received it, we rejoice. Our lives are nourished with the faith that God who began that life within us will continue that work and enable us to grow.

 Thank you, Lord God, for giving me life, and for causing that life to grow.

Do something today that nourishes God's life within you.

■ THE DISCIPLINE OF LIFE

1 Cor. 9:24-27:   "No, I beat my body and make it
my slave so that after I have preached to others,
I myself will not be disqualified for the prize" (v. 27).

The national anthem began to play, and as we
watched, a gold medal was placed around the neck
of the athlete. We rejoiced with the athlete in his
victory, knowing that it had been won at great price.

In his letter to the Corinthians, Paul wrote about
Christian discipline. At first that may seem odd—the
apostle of grace writing about the work of discipline.
But Paul realized that to be a disciple of Christ one
had to be disciplined in one's life.

For the growing Christian there is the inward
discipline, which includes Bible study, prayer, and
meditation. There is also the outward discipline of a
strong moral and ethical life, and a life of service
to others. None of these comes easily.

The idea of discipline does not take away from
God's grace. We are still saved by grace through
faith and then empowered for disciplined lives of
service to others.

 Father, I don't like discipline, because it is hard.
But it is the path you call me to. Help me to
live a disciplined life.

**Today begin a specific discipline, such as Bible study
or a service activity.**

■ THE WORST OF SINNERS

1 Tim. 1:12-17:   "Christ Jesus came into the world to save sinners—of whom I am the worst" (v. 15).

D ave was sitting in a Christian fellowship group, discussing Christian growth. He made this observation, "I feel that my life has been changing, and I have given up some pet sins like smoking, swearing, and an uncontrolled temper. But the longer I walk with Christ, the more I realize I am a sinner, and the more I need his grace."

It is common in Christian circles to believe that Christian growth is seen only in the outward life. Growth is linked only to the discipline of Bible study and prayer, the molding of character, and the giving up of specific sins. Yet there is also an inward growth.

This inward growth is a revelation of who we are. We are by nature people who go against God. We rebel against his lordship in our lives and seek to put ourselves on God's throne. Even at our best, we are not worthy of God's love and our salvation. We must rely more and more on God's grace.

Christians do not come to God with the proud boast of, "I gave up another sin." Rather, we come with the confession, "Lord, I am a sinner. Forgive me."

 Heavenly Father, as I grow in my Christian life, help me always to realize my need for your grace.

In your prayers include a specific time of confession.

■ DEDICATING LIFE TO SERVICE

Rom. 12:1-2: "Therefore, I urge you, brothers, in view of God's mercy, to offer your bodies as living sacrifices, holy and pleasing to God" (v. 1).

D ale's life was stretched to the limit. He worked long hard hours at his job. He willingly gave much of his time to his wife and two daughters. Then there were his service club and church activities. The days seemed about four hours too short.

When the pastor of Dale's church stopped by to ask him if he would run for the council, Dale had to refuse. "I just don't have the time to make a greater commitment to the church or to the Lord," said Dale.

"I can understand your position, Dale, and I can see you have made a wise decision," replied the pastor. "But before I go I must make one observation. When you run for church council or serve in any activity of the church, you aren't making a greater commitment to the Lord. As a Christian you have committed everything to the Lord already. An extra church activity is just one way to express that commitment."

Paul called growing Christians to dedicate their bodies as a living sacrifice. He was not calling them to get more involved in the church. He was exhorting them to realize that every activity of their lives is an expression of their faith and commitment to Jesus Christ.

 "Take my life, and let it be consecrated, Lord, to thee."

Make a list of how you serve God in your work, your family, and your outside activities.

■ BEING PATIENT WITH PEOPLE

Col. 3:1-14: "Therefore as God's chosen people, holy and dearly loved, clothe yourselves with compassion, kindness, humility, gentleness and patience" (v. 12).

Jane walked into the store, and it seemed as if the entire world had been turned upside down. All the merchandise had been moved. On top of that, there were workmen all around, and saws were buzzing and hammers ringing. As Jane walked through the store, she spotted a large sign which read, "Please excuse the inconvenience! We are remodeling."

Jane entered her church for her Sunday adult class. She bumped into a woman sporting a button that read, "PBPGIFWMY."

"What does that mean?" Jane asked.

"Oh," came the reply, "it stands for 'Please Be Patient, God Isn't Finished With Me Yet.' "

What a beautiful insight into the work of the Holy Spirit! Christians are under construction. The Holy Spirit is moving in our lives to form us into the image of Jesus Christ. But in no one has the remodeling been completed. We need to be patient. God still is at work.

 Lord, you work in my life and enable me to grow and to change. Help me to be patient as you do the same work in the lives of others.

List ways people have needed to be patient with you. What are some ways you can be patient with them?

■ LOVING IN THE MIDST OF HATE

John 13:1-13:   "Having loved his own who were in the world, he now showed them the full extent of his life" (v. 1).

Dave had been hurt by Len through a shady business deal on Len's part. It had cost Dave several thousand dollars. As a result, Dave had a great deal of anger and dislike for Len.

Now Len was in trouble. He had started a business, but he had been robbed several times, and during the last robbery his building had been set on fire.

Dave's first thought was to go up to Len and say, "You got exactly what you deserve!" Instead, he found himself walking up to Len and saying, "Len, I heard what happened, and I came by to say I'm sorry about it. I also want to offer you the use of my equipment until you get back on your feet—no charge, of course."

Tears came to Len's eyes. He reached out and shook Dave's hand and said, "Thanks!"

Just before telling of the Last Supper, John wrote that Jesus loved his disciples. He even loved Judas, whom he knew was going to betray him.

Growing Christians don't follow their "natural reactions" and try to get back at someone. We are called to do the impossible, to love in the midst of hate. With God's Spirit in our lives we can do it.

 Lord Jesus, you loved me even when I turned my back on you. Help me to love others.

In forgiveness and love seek to repair a broken relationship.

■ PRAISING THE LORD

Phil. 4:4-7: "Rejoice in the Lord always. I will say it again: Rejoice!" (v. 4).

Dorothy had started a business of her own. For the first two years the business was quite successful. Then the recession hit, and business fell off. Dorothy's new business didn't have the staying power, and Dorothy had to file for bankruptcy.

Some of Dorothy's friends from church came to console her. After a short conversation one of her friends piped up, "Well, Dorothy, in a situation like this you just have to praise the Lord."

Dorothy was both angered and shocked. "Praise the Lord for losing my business? That's absurd!" she snapped.

There are some Christians who encourage everyone to praise the Lord *for* all things, but they miss Paul's point. Christians are to praise the Lord *in* all things. We praise the Lord for *who he is,* not for what has happened.

Even in the midst of tragedy we can still praise the Lord. We can praise Christ because he still loves us and has chosen us to be his. We can praise the Lord because he is God almighty. We can praise Christ because he has the ability to take the bad in our lives and turn it for good.

In all situations of life we can praise the Lord, who walks with us through them.

 Praise you, Father, for you are God, Creator of the universe.

Set aside five minutes of your prayer time for praise.

■ GIVING THANKS

1 Thess. 5:15-22:   "Give thanks in all circumstances, for this is God's will for you in Christ
Jesus" (v. 18).

P eter had received five dollars from his uncle.
"What do you say to Uncle Jack, Peter?" quizzed
his mother.

"Thank you," Peter said, as he ran to show the
other kids his prize.

We have all been in Peter's shoes, with parents
reminding us of the "magic words." They hoped that
we would be polite and thankful when we received
a gift, even when we were out of their sight.

Often we forget this lesson in our prayers. We use
our prayer time to list our many needs, and we remind
God of his promise to provide for us. Occasionally we
also pray about the needs of close friends, or of
Christian programs. But we may forget to give
thanks.

In his explanation to the Apostles' Creed, Luther
wrote that God has given us, "clothing and food,
house and family, and all I need for daily life." When
we stop and think about it, that is a lot to be thankful
for. We need to remember what our parents told us
about saying "thank you," and apply it to our
relationship with God.

 Father, you have blessed me in so many ways
. . . and you have given me so much. Thank you.

**Make a list of what God has given you to remind you
to be thankful.**

64

■ PERSISTENT PRAYER

Luke 18:1-8: "Then Jesus told his disciples a parable to show them that they should always pray and not give up" (v. 1).

The old woman's voice was weak with age, but her eyes sparkled and her grip was strong. She had the commanding presence of a saint who had been through life.

During a brief conversation she confided, "I have been praying for a revival in this church for 50 years. After all those years, I can now see the Lord answering my prayer." What a testimony of faith is this woman's prayer life!

Too often we are people of the instant *now*. What we see, we want, and we want it *now*. When we pray, we expect God to answer our prayers immediately. When God doesn't, we often give up the prayer and mumble to ourselves that he wasn't listening, or that our prayer wasn't God's will.

The Bible encourages persistent prayer. That is a part of a growing Christian's life. We seek to know God's will and to pray that that will be done. We pray for the church, for the hungry of the world, for peace and for justice, and we continue to pray until our prayers are answered.

Our God is gracious and loving. God hears our prayers and seeks to answer them. With this knowledge, we pray persistently and wait expectantly.

 Lord, teach me to pray and to wait expectantly for your answer.

Write down two or three prayer requests and pray for them until they are answered.

■ HOPE IN THE MIDST OF TRAGEDY

Job 19:23-29: "I know that my Redeemer lives" (v. 25).

Mary stood at the side of the grave, stunned. Her husband had been killed in a car accident. She missed him, and she was angry that he had left her. She had two children and a job that wouldn't support them. She couldn't keep on going. It was a hopeless situation, and she was scared.

Job faced a similar situation. In one day he lost his children and wealth. Job asked himself, "Why?" He became angry and depressed. In modern jargon, he went through the process of grief.

In one area Job is an example to the growing Christian. Throughout his suffering he always clung to a seed of faith, for he stated, "I know that my Redeemer lives."

Everyone goes through a situation in which there seems to be no light at the end of the tunnel. The situation seems hopeless. Yet it is at these times that God gives us the precious gift of hope. God assures us of his presence in our lives and his ability to care for us.

As Christians, we have hope not in ourselves, nor in anything that the world has to offer. Instead, our hope is in a living and all-powerful God.

 Sometimes I do not have any hope, O God. Give me your gift of hope and help me to place my faith in you.

Be of service and encouragement to someone in a hopeless situation.

■ HAVING PATIENCE WITH GOD

Isa. 40:27-31:   "But those who hope in the Lord
will renew their strength" (v. 31).

T he young mother was walking to the park with her
young son. The boy, about four years old, was
anxious to get to the park. He would run ahead of
his mother and wave her on, "Come on, mom, hurry
up! I want to go on the swing set," he would cry.
The boy would then wait for his mother to catch
up before he would again run ahead and urge her
to hurry up.

The scene is similar to our relationship with God
at times. We are like small children anxious to have
things happen quickly. We run ahead of him and then
call back, "Hurry up, God. Get going and do
something!"

This may be our plea when we desire to have
people respond to our witness of faith in Jesus Christ.
This may be our plea when we don't seem to be
growing fast enough in our Christian lives. And this
may be our plea when we see things that need to be
changed.

It is good to know that God is like the young
mother. God has his own pace, but God accomplishes
his will. Instead of running ahead of God all the
time, we can sit down and wait. While we wait,
our strength and our faith will be renewed.

 Lord, you are so patient with me when I stumble
and fall or turn my back on you. Help me to
be patient with you as you act in my life and
in the lives of others.

**Make a list of your prayer requests. Date the list, then
add the date when they are answered.**

■ WE'RE A NEW CREATION

2 Cor. 5:16-21: "Therefore, if anyone is in Christ, he is a new creation; the old has gone, the new has come!" (v. 17).

On a hot summer night Ben walked into his small apartment. "Karen," he said, "let's go for a walk and stop by the ice cream shop."

Karen had a quizzical look on her face. "Good idea, but who's going to watch our two-week-old son?"

Ben was sheepish as he replied, "I completely forgot about him. I keep wanting to do things the way we used to. I need to remember that things have changed."

Things are constantly changing in our lives. Our bodies, thoughts, and ideas change. We graduate, we marry, we move, we change jobs, we meet new friends—all are changes in our lives.

Yet none of these changes compare to the change that Paul talks about. When God touches our lives and gives us salvation, we become a new creation. The old life lived in rebellion against God is destroyed. A new life arises. We no longer live only to survive, we live to serve. We don't focus our love on ourselves, we focus it on others. We don't just get, we give. Part of a growing Christian's life is the discovery of how vast the change is in our lives.

 Thank you, Holy Spirit, for making me a new creation. Help me to live in the newness.

List ways that you are a new person because of what God has done in your life.

■ LIVING THE COMMANDMENTS

John 15:5-17: "My command is this: Love each other as I have loved you" (v. 12).

A small boy approached his mother sobbing.

"What's wrong?" she asked.

"I don't have any money to buy you a birthday present," came the sobbing reply.

The mother responded. "Oh, I know something you can do. You can be well-behaved and obey me. That's the nicest gift you could ever give me."

Christians are often confronted with the problem of expressing their love of God. At times the greatest of choirs are inadequate to sing of such love. Words are unable to express the depth of the love, and worship services fail to meet the challenge. There is something that always expresses a Christian's love of God: a life lived in obedience to God's commandments.

Many mistake this to mean that we yoke ourselves up to numerous do's and don'ts. But the commandments of God are summed up in one big DO—Do love!"

When the Spirit opens our eyes, we see countless ways to live the commandments. There are so many people in need of love. We do not live in love for our salvation or for some award at church. We live in love to express our love of God.

 Lord Jesus, help me express my love for you by loving others.

Choose one person in your life and think of a new way to express love to that person.

■ TRUSTING PEOPLE

1 Cor. 12:25-26: "If one part suffers, every part suffers with it; if one part is honored, every part rejoices with it" (v. 26).

George Miller lay silently in the hospital bed. He was in the cardiac care unit after having suffered a severe heart attack.

In his recovery, George was at first afraid to trust his heart. He felt that any exertion would trigger another attack. But little by little he saw he could get back to a normal life. Later George would trust his heart in vigorous exercise.

There are times when other members of the body of Christ hurt us, and we withdraw our trust from them. Often we never renew our trust in them, because we're afraid they might hurt us again. This lack of trust hurts both us and them, and the entire church suffers.

We need to work together in trust. Where trust has diminished, it needs to be built up. This can be done by living in forgiveness, fellowship, faith, and hope. At times trust is not easy, yet if the body is to be healthy, it is a necessity.

As the body of Christ we can be crippled by doubt and inward fears, or we can go forth in trust and proclaim the good news.

 Lord, you trust me to spread your good news to those around me. Help me to trust others and to grow in my trust of them.

Think of a small way to begin to build up your trust in someone who has hurt you.

■ SEEKING DIRECTION

Ps. 119:103-105: "Your word is a lamp to my feet and a light for my path" (v. 105).

S cott needed some guidance in his life. He was given an opportunity to advance in his company. At the same time he was offered a position with another company. In the decision he was about to make, he wanted to do God's will, but he was not sure what God's will was. Scott turned to God's Word.

God's Word is his power at work within us. It is a light, and it gives us direction, even in our modern lives.

God moves in our lives and directs us through meditation, prayer, and Bible study. God guides us through the counsel and fellowship of believers. Trusted friends with their insight are used by God to set us on the correct path.

We need no mystical appearance in order to be guided. God uses what is already available—the Word and other Christians.

God does seek to guide us in our daily lives. The Word is our light. Perhaps God does not guide us in what soap we buy, but certainly God guides us in our job, family, friends, and areas of service.

 Lord, you have set a path before me. Help me to see it and to willingly walk it.

Describe how God guided you in a past decision.

■ AWARE OF GOD'S PRESENCE

1 Kings 19:9-14: "After the earthquake came a fire, but the Lord was not in the fire. And after the fire came a gentle whisper" (v. 12).

M ike awoke to the shuffling of his two children as they prepared for school. Breakfast contained not only a piece of toast, but final instructions to the children on behavior and pick-up times. At the office there were hundreds of questions, and the phone wouldn't stop ringing. After work there was television and a short chat with his wife before going to bed.

As they sat together on the sofa, Mike turned to his wife and said, "You know, I just don't feel God's presence in my life anymore."

We may not need earthquakes or fires to do an effective job of drowning out the voice of God. Sometimes we just can't hear him through all the static.

A gentle whisper assured Elijah of God's presence and power. God comes to us in the same way. God speaks to us and assures us of his presence during our meditation and prayer and when we read the Word. God doesn't force himself on us. God waits until we are open, and then speaks.

God is present with us at all times, but an awareness of that presence often comes in our quiet times.

 Lord, in the rat race of life, help me to be quiet so that you may speak and assure me of your presence.

Set aside a specific time to be still before the Lord.

■ LAGGING ENTHUSIASM

Matt. 25:1-13: ''The foolish ones said to the wise, 'Give us some of your oil; our lamps are going out' '' (v. 8).

The young boy received an electronic game for his birthday. For several days all one could hear in the house was the ping and squeal of the game. After two weeks the game was played only in the evening. After six months the game had found its way into the corner of the boy's closet.

Most of us have experienced a similar lag of enthusiasm in various areas of our lives—even in our Christian commitment. We begin to feel like those foolish virgins who did not take along extra oil and ran out.

It is difficult to sustain a high level of enthusiasm over a long period of time. When our enthusiasm lags, we realize that it is a part of the growing process. At this time, enthusiasm needs to be reinforced with a disciplined commitment.

We Christians are like long-distance runners and not sprinters. We need to pace ourselves. Our life with Christ goes beyond the time when the newness wears off. It is for a lifetime.

It is also important for us to cultivate our enthusiasm. We do this through worship, fellowship, prayer, Bible study, and service.

 Lord, with your strength, help me to go the distance.

List ways you inspire enthusiasm for yourself in your favorite hobbies and sports.

■ CELEBRATE

Psalm 150:   "Let everything that has breath praise the Lord!" (v. 6).

As they drove to a party, Wes complained to Wendy, "I sure don't feel like celebrating tonight. That repair bill for the washing machine just ruined my day."

"Well, I'm not going to let it spoil my evening," replied Wendy. "I know that it put a dent in our finances, but we've made it through before, and we'll do it again. Besides, there is so much to be thankful about."

It is tempting to go through life feeling like Wes did at that moment. When anything bad happens in our lives, we respond to it by complaining and depression. Life turns into something to be endured rather than something to be experienced and enjoyed. We promise ourselves that we will celebrate when everything is going our way.

The Bible exhorts us to praise the Lord and to celebrate. This is the daily practice of the Christian and not something that occurs only when things are going well.

We are able to celebrate because our Lord reigns. We have new life in Christ. We have meaning and purpose in our lives. No matter what our situation, we have much to celebrate.

 Lord, help me to live with a spirit of celebration even when my feelings are low. May your praise be always on my lips.

Today find a way to celebrate the life you have in Jesus Christ.

■ NULLIFYING GOD'S WORD

Matt. 15:3-9: "Thus you nullify the word of God for the sake of your tradition" (v. 6).

The yellow caution sign said, "Slippery When Wet." Doug didn't think that sign applied to him, even if it was raining. He entered the curve with too much speed, lost control of his car, and went into the ditch.

Ken noticed the label on his sweater, "Wash in cold water only," but he did not pay any attention to it. He threw the sweater, along with the other clothes, into the hot water. When he pulled his sweater out from the wash, it was ruined.

People often ignore the messages they receive. They pass them off as not being important, or as pertaining only to someone else.

It is tempting for Christians to treat the Scripture this way. We open our Bible, but as we read it, we do not believe that it has anything to say to us. When we encounter a troubling verse, we explain it away as not being applicable to our situation and time, or as being too revolutionary to follow in our lives.

The Word of God gives life, but only to those who sense they need life and are open to being touched by the message it contains.

 Holy Spirit, help me to hear what you have to say to me.

Write down ways you explain away or nullify God's Word.

■ BOLDLY ENTERING GOD'S PRESENCE

Heb. 10:19-25:   "Let us draw near to God with a
sincere heart in full assurance of faith" (v. 22).

It was an important family function, and Jane wanted
very much to be there. But she had already used up
her vacation time. If she were to go to the event, she
would need to ask her boss for more time off.

For two days Jane worked up courage to go to her
boss. She made countless starts, until with a burst of
determination she marched to the boss's office and
knocked on the door. She opened the door and
entered. "Ms. Paulson, I would like to have three
additional days off next month to attend an important
family get-together."

Ms. Paulson flipped through her calendar and then
looked up at Jane. "Well, I don't see why you can't
have a few days off, Jane." Jane walked out of the
office, elated that her request was granted and
amazed at how easy it had been.

Christians at times treat God as the big boss. We
do not feel free to come to him with our needs, fears,
and concerns. We tell ourselves that he probably
wouldn't be interested, or it is too small a problem to
talk to him about. But the Bible encourages us to
boldly enter his presence.

 Father, give me boldness in my prayers.

**List the needs and concerns you hesitate to pray
about. Pray about them now.**

■ DEFENDING GOD

2 Sam. 6:6-11: "Uzzah reached out and took hold of the ark of God, because the oxen stumbled" (v. 6).

In summary, my client could not be guilty of the crimes he has been charged with." The attorney concluded the defense of his client. He had made a good defense, and in all probability his client would be acquitted.

God gets blamed for many things by the people around us: famines and the injustice in the world, natural disasters like floods and earthquakes, deaths and sicknesses. As his followers we feel forced to defend God. But God does not ask us to defend him.

Uzzah thought he needed to help God out by keeping his ark from falling. In a forceful display, God pointed out that he was big enough to help himself. God did not need Uzzah's helping hand then, and he does not need our defense now.

God has called us to be witnesses, not defense attorneys. We share with those around us how we have seen God move in our lives. We bear witness to God's love in word and deed, and we let God defend himself.

 Lord, forgive me for trying to protect and defend you.

Recall incidents over the past weeks or month where your witnessing has turned into defending God.

■ THE BURDEN BEARER

Matt. 11:27-30:   "Come to me, all you who are
weary and burdened, and I will give you rest" (v. 28).

Six-year-old Ken was lugging his box of building
blocks from his room to the family room. His mother
saw him and offered to help. Asserting his
independence, Ken said, "No, I can do it myself." He
was almost to the family room when the box slipped
out of his hands. The building blocks spilled all over
the floor, and in tears Ken had to start picking
them up.

We laugh at Ken's experience, because it is so
common. It has happened either to our children or to
us. We try to be so strong, and in the process
demonstrate our weakness.

We like to see ourselves as independent people who
are capable of running our own lives. But the burdens
of life are too great for us to bear alone. We lose our
grip on them, and they come crashing down on us.

Our Lord doesn't sit on the sidelines encouraging
us to hang tough and go it alone. Christ comes to
our aid and offers to bear our burdens. His hands are
big, and his back is strong. In him we have our help
and our rest.

  Lord Jesus, my burdens are many. Take them
so that I may rest.

**Write down the burdens you are carrying at this time.
In prayer give them over to the Lord.**

■ GET SOME REST

Mark 6:30-34: "He said to them, "Come with me by yourselves to a quiet place and get some rest'" (v. 31).

N ancy had worked hard and saved a long time for her dream vacation. Now coming back from her two-week cruise, she reminisced that it had been worth it. It was the experience of a lifetime. More than that, Nancy was relaxed and refreshed and excited about getting back into the swing of things. She was living proof of the importance of vacations.

We are constantly struggling with our schedules. There is never enough time in the day to do everything. Evidently this is an age-old problem; the disciples couldn't even grab a quick lunch.

Jesus calls to us as he did to the disciples: "Come with me to a quiet place and get some rest." We do this the same way the disciples did. They made the time. They simply went away and didn't even wait for a lull in the activity.

The Lord calls us to be poured out in service, but we also need to be filled. We are also invited to come away to a quiet place to rest and to be filled.

 I've been too busy, Lord. Enable me to take the time to be with you.

Look at your schedule. What can you change to have more time for devotions and leisure activities?

■ THE ABUNDANT LIFE

John 10:7-10: "I have come that they may have life, and have it to the full" (v. 10).

L arry passed by the new-car showroom and stared at the bright shining cars. He thought to himself, "When I'm able to trade in my old clunker for one of these, I'll have the world by the tail." Some months later, when he was able to purchase a new car, Larry discovered that life was no different.

Steve and Debbie wanted a new house. The one they had was just too small for their growing family. They thought that life would be much better when they gave up the hassels of their small home for the comfort of a larger one. When they moved into their new home, they enjoyed the larger space. But their lives had not changed—only their mortgage payments.

It is tempting to seek the abundant life in the things of this world. They are so desirable, but their abundance ends only in clutter.

Only Jesus Christ gives a truly full life, a life rich in relationship with God and overflowing with love. Nothing this world offers compares to it.

 Thank you, Lord, for giving me a full life.

Make a list of the ways your life has become full through your life with God.

■ THE PATH OF CHRIST

John 14:1-7: "I am the way and the truth and the life. No one comes to the Father except through me" (v. 6).

The Evans family was on the way to watch a professional ball game. They were excited about the game and the trip to the city. But they had never been to the city before, and they did not know where the stadium was.

They stopped at a service station on the outskirts of the city and asked the attendant for directions. Mr. Evans wrote them down on a piece of paper. An hour later they were hopelessly lost.

They stopped by another station and explained their predicament. After listening to their story the attendant said, "I'm headed out that way on a service call. Why don't you just follow me.'" Within minutes they were at the stadium.

The path of life can be confusing at times. Many books have been written to help us find the way. There are many people who are willing to give advice. But only one, Jesus Christ, takes us by the hand, walks with us, and leads us through.

 Thank you, Jesus, that you are my path through life.

Remember when you played "Follow the Leader"? How is that like your Christian life?

■ MEASURING CHRISTIAN GROWTH

Matt. 5:17-20:   "Unless your righteousness surpasses that of the Pharisees and teachers of the law, you will certainly not enter the kingdom of heaven" (v. 20).

I t was a yearly tradition. On the first day of school, mom would back the children up to the door frame one by one and mark their heights. As the years passed, they could easily see how they were growing. It was fun to see the difference in a year.

Many Christians would like to be able to measure their growth like that. But spiritual growth is hard to measure.

When Christians do attempt to measure their growth, they often use the wrong measuring stick. They begin to use the things they do as an indicator. They tally up activities such as church committees and Bible studies as marks of growth. Or they take pride in the "sinful" things they don't do. This is the same measuring stick that the Pharisees used.

As the Spirit moves in our lives, we are transformed and molded into the image of Christ. Christian growth comes not in what we do, but in who we are. Growth is a process of being changed by God—being transformed into loving people. This growth is not measured in the comfort of our churches but in the struggles of life.

 Father, mold me into the image of your Son.

Ask a friend who has gone through a struggle with you how they see that you have grown as a Christian.

■ PRAYING FOR OTHERS

Eph. 6:18-20:   ''Always keep on praying for all the saints'' (v. 18).

Honey, am I glad you're home!" came the yell from the kitchen as Fred walked in the door. As his wife came to give him a hello kiss, she said, "I found a sale on kids' jeans, so I bought some. But I overdrew the checking account to do it. Dan was hurt in gym class today. Mary may have a chance to go on a science field trip, and Josh needs your help with his bike."

After supper Fred read from the Bible and from a family devotional booklet. The family joined in a hymn, and then bowed their heads in prayer. Their prayers centered around the needs of the family. They included help with the finances, thanks for protecting Dan, blessings on Mary, and help for Josh in school. Following the Lord's Prayer the family members each went their own way.

Yet there is so much more to pray about. There are the missionaries in far-off lands and nearby cities. There are people struggling for their freedom, and some who are struggling to survive. There are people who are sick and others who need God's love and salvation.

In our prayers we have the opportunity and the privilege of praying not only for ourselves but also for the world around us.

 Forgive me, Lord, when I use my time of prayer only for selfish reasons. Help me to keep on praying for others.

Pray for five people around you and five world events.

■ BE STILL BEFORE GOD

Ps. 46:8-11:   "Be still, and know that I am God"
(v. 10).

The young couple were on their first date together. They enjoyed being with each other, but at times their conversation lagged and there were long periods of silence. During these times they were both uncomfortable and constantly shifted in their seats.

What a contrast between this couple and an older couple who had been married several years. In the older couple's life together there had been many times of silence. They shared such silences together and communicated their love for each other without words. These silent times were special, more so even than times of conversation.

In our relationship with God we are often like the young couple. We are uncomfortable with silence. We enter into God's presence and immediately begin to list our requests. During a pause our minds flit from work, to family, to church, to neighbors. If the pause becomes lengthy, we feel that we have prayed enough and go back to our daily routine.

The Lord says to us, "Be still, and know that I am God." What a privilege for us to enter into God's presence in silence, and in that silence to listen to God reveal his love and power to us.

 Help me in silence to experience you as God.

During your prayer time take five or ten minutes to be totally silent before God.

84

■ PRAYING WHERE YOU ARE

Matt. 26:36-46:   ''My Father, if it is possible, may this cup be taken from me. Yet not as I will, but as you will'' (v. 39).

Brian came home and confessed to his wife Mary, "I don't know how to pray about this situation. They're talking about layoffs at work. I'm concerned about my job, and I am also concerned about the other guys."

Mrs. Clemens picked up the phone. Her brother was on the line. Her father had suffered a major stroke, and his chances were 50/50. "How should I pray?" Mrs. Clemens asked. "I don't know," came the reply.

We all enter situations which provoke the question, "How should I pray?" The answer is simply to pray where you're at. All too often our prayers become a series of work orders for the Lord. We say in effect, "I have analyzed the situation, Lord, and this is what needs to be done."

The struggle of Jesus in the garden is a powerful example of prayer. Prayer is conversation and sharing. It is struggling with a problem and communicating that struggle. In prayer it is permissible to share our worries, concerns, hopes, and fears. We can list the possible answers and then put it all in the hands of the Lord. Prayer is more than lists and work orders. It is sharing our life where we are at.

 Thank you, Lord, that you are willing to share in my struggles and challenges.

Look at your prayers. Have they become a series of work orders for God to accomplish? Try just sharing where you're at.

■ WITNESSES FOR CHRIST

Matt. 28:16-20:   "Therefore go and make disciples of all nations, baptizing them in the name of the Father and of the Son and of the Holy Spirit" (v. 19).

There was the screeching of brakes, then the sickening crunch of metal as the two cars came together. Luckily no one was hurt, but the cars were both badly damaged.

Within minutes police officers were at the scene. While one directed traffic around the accident, another took statements from the drivers and from those who witnessed the accident.

One of the witnesses had already made up his mind whose fault it was. When he began to tell the police officer his opinion, the officer shook his head and stopped the man. "Sir, that is not what I want to know," the officer said. "I just want to know what you saw happen."

When we bear witness to our faith in Jesus Christ, we are much like the witnesses of the car accident. We do not need to pass any judgment and get into an argument on what is right and what is wrong. We do not need to defend God or God's Word. We simply need to share what we have seen and heard and felt in our individual lives and in the corporate life of the church.

We are called to be witnesses, not judges, defenders, or salespeople. The Holy Spirit takes our words and creates faith in the hearer. The Spirit is the one who brings them into a relationship with God.

 Lord Jesus, give me the boldness to be your witness.

Share your faith story with someone close to you.

■ FREEDOM IN CHRIST

Gal. 5:13-17: "Do not use your freedom to indulge the sinful nature; rather, serve one another in love" (v. 13).

Free at last, free at last. Thank God Almighty, I'm free at last." For Martin Luther King Jr., this statement indicated freedom from social inequality and freedom to live in peace. When the Bible talks about freedom it means more.

Christ has set us free. He has set us free from the effects of our sin—free from our bondage to sin and from our separation from God.

For the Christian this is good news. We no longer need to occupy our time attempting to make up for our sins. We no longer need to engage in the hopeless struggle against our sinfulness and our rebellion. We no longer need to live in loneliness and anxiety.

From our bondage Christ has called us to freedom. Since we are no longer chained with the worry and anxiety that comes from our condemnation as sinful people, we are able to live for service. We are Christ's servants and ambassadors in our work, our family, our hobbies, and our leisure times. Christ has made us free.

Some use their freedom selfishly. But Christ is clear in his call to us. We are free to serve.

 Lord, in my freedom, may I live to serve you.

List ways you are using your freedom for service.

■ JUDGING MYSELF

Rom. 7:21-25:   "What a wretched man I am! Who will rescue me from this body of death?" (v. 24).

It was a sin that many people would overlook. But it had hurt several people, and John was very contrite. One by one the people involved had forgiven John. But John could not forgive himself. He had sinned, and like some harsh judge, he would not grant himself a pardon.

The core of Christian faith is that Jesus Christ died on the cross to save us from the effects of our sins—a broken relationship with God. When the good news comes to us, it is a message of love and forgiveness. But at times it is difficult to apply this message to our lives.

We are caught in the struggle of sin. We stumble and fall, and at times we fail. We agree with Paul that we are wretched people in need of deliverance.

Part of our growth is learning to live within our limitations. All of us are limited by our sinfulness. No one is perfect.

In the midst of our struggle and our cry of despair God sends his message of love and forgiveness over and over again. He offers it to us until we accept it.

 Father, thank you for your forgiveness. Help me to live each day in it.

On a slip of paper, write the areas where you judge yourself harshly. Confess them and then burn the paper. As a forgiven sinner, go and serve the Lord.

■ TIED UP WITH NEW LAWS

Gal. 5:1-6: ''It is for freedom that Christ has set us free. Stand firm, then, and do not let yourselves be burdened again by a yoke of slavery'' (v. 1).

As a child I can remember going to Aunt Clara's house. It was a terrible place. The word that one heard over and over again was, *no!* "*No,* don't sit on the couch. I just fluffed the pillows." "*No,* don't make so much noise. Uncle Al isn't feeling well." "*No,* don't ride your trike on the grass. It may leave some marks." Aunt Clara's house wasn't a place to live; it was a place to endure.

Many Christians build for themselves a house like Aunt Clara's. It is a house filled with *don'ts,* and *can'ts.* "I don't think we should get involved with the problems of those people." "I can't do that. It wouldn't be Christian." "I can't help right now. I'm late for a church meeting."

Some *can'ts* and *don'ts* are valid expressions of our faith. Many others are new laws that we tie ourselves up with.

When Jesus called us to be his disciples, he did not call us to a bunch of *don'ts.* He called us to some challenging *do's. Do* keep my commandments and love one another. *Do* serve God by serving your fellow human beings. *Do* be a good steward of my gifts to you. *Do* work for peace and justice.

We have been set free from the *Don'ts:* The freedom of the *Do's* stands before us.

 Lord, free me from the laws in which I've entangled myself. Enable me to be free in you.

List ways that you limit your freedom in Christ. How can you experience greater freedom?

■ JUDGING OTHERS

Rom. 14:13-18:   "Let us stop passing judgment on one another" (v. 13).

B ob and Shirley were driving home from church. As they drove, they discussed the worship service. "The sermon was too long today," began Bob, "and I didn't get much out of it."

"I agree," replied Shirley, "and the choir was off too."

"I was surprised to see Ken and his new wife in church," continued Bob, "so soon after his divorce from Mary."

"Yes, that is terrible," agreed Shirley. "And the Olson twins were such a disturbance in church today. I wish their mother would do something about them."

We easily fall into the habit of judging others. It is not *constructive* criticism, because it does not help the other person. It is *destructive* criticism, complaining about who they are or what they did.

There are many reasons why Christians judge others, but love is not one of them. It does not strengthen the body of Christ.

Judging others is nothing new. Paul had to deal with it in his letter to the Romans. In that letter he posed the question, "Who are we to judge?" We are not judges, we are servants. Let us be about our business.

 Father, forgive me for judging others and criticizing their service to you.

Think of a person you have judged harshly, and ask for forgiveness.

■ BEARING THE FRUIT OF THE SPIRIT

Gal. 5:22-26: "But the fruit of the Spirit is love, joy, peace, patience, kindness, goodness, faithfulness, gentleness and self-control" (vv. 22-23).

It was Steve's first season on the golf course, and he was determined to master the game. He had read a number of books on golf. Now all he had to do was transfer what he knew in his head to his game.

But try as he might, his game was a disaster. Each time he attempted to hit the ball, he would tense up and swing with the grace of a falling tree. The ball would go every way but straight. Finally in desperation Steve went to the resident pro for some help. His words were few and simple, "Don't try so hard."

At times we make Christianity into such hard work. We try so hard to be close to God and obey God's will. We try to be perfect Christians. When we do this, our Christian life goes much like Steve's golf game.

We are to *bear* the fruit of the Spirit, not *make* it. That's good news! There is not a fruit tree in the world that injures itself straining to bear fruit. The trees simply bear the fruit because that is their nature.

We have the Spirit of God within us. The Spirit is giving us new life each day and molding us into the image of Christ. As God works in our lives we begin to bear fruit.

 Holy Spirit, thank you for your work in my life. May I bear abundantly for you.

List the fruit of the Spirit that you are beginning to bear.

■ THE SPIRIT'S POWER

1 Cor. 12:4-11:   "There are different kinds of gifts, but the same Spirit" (v. 4).

R yan received a BMX bike for his birthday. It was bright red, with mag wheels, and with pads on all the tubing. Soon all the kids in the neighborhood began to pester their parents to purchase a BMX bike for them. They wanted one as nice as Ryan's.

Christians are sometimes like these children. Each of us has been given talents and abilities with which to serve the Lord. But we are often not satisfied with our talents and are envious of others and their gifts.

We like the flashy gifts. Gifts such as healing or speaking in tongues attract many. Other Christians are envious of those who can preach, teach a class, or sing a solo.

Some gifts are put down. Administration does not impress many people. Neither are sensitive and compassionate gifts like making phone calls, baking cakes, or preparing casseroles held in much esteem.

Each of us has various gifts by which we serve the Lord. Let's not put down who we are or what we have been given. Rather, let's spend our time using our gifts in the service of God.

 Lord, forgive my envy of others' gifts. Help me to use my gifts to your glory.

Make a list of the gifts you feel God has given you.

■ JESUS IS COMING

Rev. 22:17-21: ''He who testifies to these things says, 'Yes, I am coming soon.' Amen. Come, Lord Jesus'' (v. 20).

R elatives came to visit the Carpenters during the summer. They had come from a long distance and had written some months ahead to see if they could stay with the Carpenters. The Carpenters had agreed. They had cleaned and polished their home and arranged their schedule so they could entertain their guests.

"I am coming again." That's a promise Jesus made. By faith we know it is a promise he will keep. But Christianity has been divided in its response to this promise.

On the one hand, there are Christians who make this the central point of their faith. They read books and attend seminars claiming that world events are falling into patterns described by biblical prophecy.

On the other hand, there are Christians who ignore the promise. Their attitude is: "Jesus hasn't come back in 2000 years. He may not come back for another 2000. So why be concerned about it?"

Jesus announced his intentions of coming, and we, like the Carpenters, are to be prepared for his arrival. Our lives are to be in order, and we are to live each day with the expectation that he will come. One day he will!

 Lord Jesus, show me how I can be ready for your coming.

If Jesus were to return tonight, would he find you faithfully serving him in your daily life?

■ NO ONE IS SINLESS

1 John 1:5-10:   "If we claim we have not sinned, we make him out to be a liar and his word has no place in our lives" (v. 10).

Colleen was on top of the world. She had just received a promotion and a raise. At home she had a strong marriage and two beautiful children.

In her Christian life Colleen was growing. She felt a deepened faith in God. She was more disciplined in her private devotions. And she was becoming victorious over her cigarette smoking.

In her devotions Colleen would pause for a moment for confession, but she wouldn't be able to think of anything specific to confess. There were no major sins in her life.

Then one day a fellow worker walked in and sat down in Colleen's office. "I just want to say," she began, "that I was very upset by the way you lost your temper with Shirley. As a fellow worker and a fellow Christian I'm shocked at the way you sometimes treat people and the way your temper controls you." Colleen was stunned, but she had to agree that what was said was true.

Christians sometimes become complacent. We don't see any big sins in our lives, so we convince ourselves that we have no sin or no need for confession.

Yet when the Holy Spirit's light shines in our lives, our sin is obvious. We continue to need God's forgiveness.

 Father, I have sinned. Forgive me.

Who have you hurt? Ask forgiveness from those people.

■ CHRISTIAN MEEKNESS

Ps. 37:5-11: "The meek will inherit the land and enjoy great peace" (v. 11).

The speaker approached the lectern with a plaque in his hand. He showed it to the audience and said, "We'd like to present this plaque to Christine Ames for her leadership and example of service to other people."

The banquet hall erupted with applause. Chris was shocked as she arose and walked toward the lectern. As she walked, a sense of pride came over her. It had taken hard work and determination on her part. She was proud and a bit arrogant at what she had done.

Then she began to think of all the support she had received. So many people had encouraged her. There were times when she wanted to give up, but then someone had said just the right word. She began to realize that she was part of a team. It was their award. She accepted the award with thankfulness and meekness.

We sometimes become arrogant in our Christian lives. We have many talents and abilities which give us a strong ministry. But we forget how our ministry is part of the church's witness.

In meekness we see that all we have is a gift from God. And God's work is done not just by us but by others with us.

 Father, forgive me when I become arrogant over my service to you. May I in meekness remember your movement in my life.

Thank the people around you for their support and help.

■ FOLLOWING A DIFFERENT PATH

Acts 21:7-14: "When we heard this, we and the people there pleaded with Paul not to go up to Jerusalem" (v. 12).

Jeff was disturbed by the government's policy toward South America. He felt the policies were wrong and contributed to the deaths of many people. Jeff sent many letters to his congressmen stating his beliefs.

The vice-president was scheduled to speak at a convention to be held in the city where Jeff lived. Jeff decided that he needed to demonstrate his beliefs when the vice-president spoke. He began to contact people he knew with similar views and to arrange a peaceful demonstration outside the auditorium.

When Jeff's parents heard of his plans, they were very upset. They felt that a Christian's duty was to support the government. His fellow workers were concerned that Jeff's action would block a promotion for him. And his girlfriend thought it was simply a waste of time.

Jeff listened to all the arguments. They had some valid points, but this was something he felt he needed to do. As a Christian he could not sit back. He had to act.

There are times when we, like Paul and Jeff, must follow our inner voice rather than the counsel of others. It's a difficult decision, yet one which must be made.

 Father, may I always follow your guiding Spirit.

List times when you sensed the Holy Spirit inwardly guiding you. Has this ever been against the advice of others?

■ DISCIPLESHIP COSTS

Luke 9:23-27:   "For whoever wants to save his life will lose it, but whoever loses his life for me will save it" (v. 24).

An old musician near the end of his career performed a concert. He was very talented, and the music he played was magic. At the end of his performance he received a standing ovation.

Backstage after the performance the musician was met by a young admirer who said, "I'd give my life to be able to play like that." Without blinking the musician said, "That's exactly what it cost me," and he turned and walked away.

In the Christian church we celebrate God's free grace. By his grace he has made us members of his family. He has filled us with the Holy Spirit. He has given us an abundant life. He has called us to be his disciples.

Though our salvation through Christ is free, our discipleship is costly. We lose the life that wants to live in opposition to God. The part of us that desires to be served is given up and replaced by a person who serves others. Each day we encounter situations in which we must deny ourselves in order to answer the call of Christ.

When Christ said, "I go to prepare a place for you," it cost him his life. When he calls to us and says, "Follow me and I will make you fishers of men," it costs us our lives.

 Lord, help me to be willing to pay the price of discipleship.

Write down what your discipleship to Jesus Christ is costing you.

■ PROBLEMS IN PRAYER

James 4:1-3: "When you ask, you do not receive, because you ask with wrong motives, that you may spend what you get on your pleasures" (v. 3).

Diane had formed the habit of getting up 15 minutes early to pray. When she had first started, it had been a refreshing experience.

Recently her prayer life was drying up. It was harder to get up those 15 minutes early to pray. The time wasn't refreshing, and her prayers did not seem to be answered.

Diane was concerned and took a look at her time of prayer. Over the past two or three weeks she had prayed about her need to furnish her apartment, some new clothes, a raise, and help on her job. It occurred to her that her prayer list looked more like a shopping list than anything else. Basically it read, "I need and I want."

Determined to make a change, Diane began the next morning with a time of thanksgiving for all that the Lord had given her. She also had a time of prayer for those who were in need. There were those who were sick and a neighbor who had been laid off. There was a friend with an alcohol problem.

Her prayer life quickly changed. Once again it had life in it, and the lines of communication were cleared.

Often in our prayers, we heed the words of James. We do not receive because we pray wrongly and only for our own pleasures.

 Lord, teach me to pray.

Pray for five people who are in need.

■ MEETING THE NEEDS OF OTHERS

Luke 10:29-37: "Which of these do you think was a neighbor to the man who fell into the hands of robbers?" (v. 36).

The old woman was crippled with a severe case of arthritis. She moved slowly, and each movement was accompanied by pain. "I can't do much to serve the Lord feeling like this," she thought as she prepared a casserole for a new neighbor.

The 10-year-old girl had the same thoughts. "I can't do anything to serve God. I am only 10 years old." She joined a team of youngsters in an "adopt a grandparent program" at the local nursing home.

"I can't serve the Lord," thought the teenage boy, as he sat down by the new kid in school and introduced himself.

"I'm too busy at work to do anything for the Lord," thought the executive as he drove to work. On his way he spotted a car with its hood up. Since his hobby was fixing up old cars, he pulled over to see if he could be of any help.

Most Christians feel they are ill-prepared and inadequate to serve the Lord and minister to other people. They equate ministry with preaching or counseling or teaching a Bible class. Meeting the needs of others and ministering to them is not difficult or technical. Most people simply need love, kindness, compassion, and respect.

 Lord, I am able to serve you. Here I am, use me.

Do what you are able to minister to a person who is in need.

■ AS THEY WERE ABLE

2 Cor. 8:1-7: "They gave as much as they were able, and even beyond their ability" (v. 3).

Honey, how much should I put in the offering envelope this Sunday?"

"I don't know," came the reply. "We have about $40 to last us for the month. I suppose we can spare $2 or $3."

This scene is played in countless households. Many Christians who are concerned about the mission of the church have not seriously thought about what they give to that mission.

There are some established principles, though, which help the growing Christian to handle money and give a portion of it to the mission of the church.

Giving is first *deliberate*. Christians determine the amount of money they will give to the church over a specific period of time.

Giving is also *off the top*. It's all too tempting to see what's left after the bills. The growing Christian gives first and then pays the bills.

Finally, giving is *growing*. Growing Christians give an increasing percentage of their income. This year it might be 5%. Next year the aim may be for 7%, with the goal of giving 15% five years in the future.

Giving is *a discipline* and is part of the life of the growing Christian.

 Lord, you have given me much. Help me to use it wisely.

Figure out what percentage of your income you are giving. Think about increasing it.

■ A MEMBER OF THE BODY

1 Cor. 12:14-26:   "For the body is not made up of one part but of many" (v. 14).

While Tanya was sitting watching television one evening, she thought she heard a noise. Her mind sounded the alarm. In response, her heart started to beat faster. Her muscles tensed. Her ears strained to hear another sound, and her eyes attempted to pierce the darkness. Within moments her body was poised to work together to flee from danger.

In his letter to the Corinthians Paul reminds us that we are each a part of the body of Christ. The mission of the church is a team effort. We work together to accomplish the call God has given us. If scandal or division takes place in one area of the church, the entire church suffers the hurt and shame. When one area of ministry is effective, the entire church shares the honor.

Many a Christian tries to be a one person team. They singlehandedly attempt to proclaim the gospel. They spurn the help of others, and they insist on being in control. They have lost the vision that they are members of Christ's body, and the body hurts because of it.

The call of Christ is too challenging, and the mission of Christ is too vast, to be handled by one member of the body. The body must be united in its ministry and work like a team to the glory of God.

 Forgive me, Father, when I forget that I am simply a member of your body and a part of the team.

List ways you can be more of a team player.

■ GOD WORKS THROUGH COMMITTEES

Acts 6:1-7: "Brothers, choose seven men from among you who are known to be full of the Spirit and wisdom" (v. 3).

That's a great idea, Jill," said the pastor. "I think you should bring it up to the evangelism committee and see if they will work with you on it."

Two weeks later Jill returned from the committee meeting very upset. "What's the matter?" quizzed her husband.

"Oh, they thought it was a good idea, all right," said Jill, "but they don't have it in their budget. It will have to wait until next year. I sure don't know why God invented committees!"

Many people echo Jill's words. We get good ideas, and we want to run with them and see them work. When we encounter a committee, our progress is slowed and sometimes brought to a standstill. Other times our great ideas are modified. We begin to see committees as obstacles and enemies.

Yet God uses committees. In Christ's body, the church, they become a check-and-balance system that does not allow one person to use the church for his or her own purpose. They provide for a more unified ministry of the church, and they recruit more than one or two people for the task.

In our impatience, committees can become our enemies. But God does use them to proclaim the word here on earth.

 Forgive me, Lord, for my impatience with committees. Help me to work with them rather than against them.

Attend a committee meeting. If possible serve on a committee for at least one year.

■ THE TIME BUDGET

Eph. 5:15-21: ". . . making the most of every opportunity . . ." (v. 6).

Chuck and Michelle sat down at the end of the month to look over their budget. They had done a good job staying in their budget. They had overspent in only one area and had underspent in another to balance it out.

Many people have used a budget. Budgets enable us to live within the income the Lord has given us. They help us use money wisely.

Another area where a budget is needed is our time. We have only a certain amount of it. As Christians we are challenged to live our lives, making the most of every opportunity.

Each of us has been given a 24-hour day. But we use that gift in different ways. Some bunch up their budget of time and spend it all on work. Then they have to cut back on family or leisure time. Others spend time in work, family, and leisure, but they neglect service. Some have time to "kill," while others can't find enough of it.

Time is a precious gift, more precious than money. We are challenged to use it wisely, and to use it to God's glory. To do this we cannot live it thoughtlessly, but we must budget it wisely.

 Lord, help me to manage my time so that it witnesses to your glory.

Make a list of ways you waste time, or overbudget your time. What changes need to be made?

■ MEMORIZING GOD'S WORD

Ps. 119:9-16:   "I have hidden your word in my heart that I might not sin against you" (v. 11).

The car left the road and rolled down the embankment. Cathy lost consciousness when she hit her head on the steering wheel. When she awoke, she was in an ambulance on her way to the hospital. As she lay in the ambulance, the words, "The Lord is my shield and my strength," came to her, and she was comforted.

Tom was laid off from his job. He went home to share the news with his wife. As they talked about the future, they realized that there were quite a few possibilities. They just didn't know which one to take. Then both of them remembered a verse they had learned in Sunday school: "Ask and you will receive, seek and you will find, knock and it will be opened to you." They knew that the Lord was with them.

We believe that God reveals himself to us and speaks to us through the Bible. Many are diligent in reading the Bible daily and studying it. But few have done what the psalmist did and hidden the word in their hearts.

God uses his Word to touch our lives. That Word is more available if it is hidden in our hearts rather than confined to some printed pages.

 Lord, help me to discipline myself and to memorize your Word.

On a piece of paper write down a passage of Scripture you want to memorize. During your free time memorize the verse.

■ HANDLING ANGER

Eph. 4:25-32:   " 'In your anger do not sin': Do not
let the sun go down while you are still angry" (v. 26).

T he moment Lee walked through the door you
could tell he was upset. The door slammed shut, and
his wife did not receive the usual hello kiss.

One of Lee's fellow workers had dumped the blame
of an unfilled order squarely on him. It was an unjust
accusation, but Lee was called on the carpet for it.
Now Lee was taking his anger out on everyone. His
wife, defending herself, told him that a Christian
shouldn't get so angry.

Lee faced a problem that every Christian faces.
People and situations in life make us angry. As
Christians how do we handle our anger?

First, its necessary to realize that anger, in itself, is
not a sin. Anger is a natural emotion we all have.

Confrontation is one way to handle anger. If
someone made you angry, tell him or her about it. If
a situation made you angry, you can seek to
change it.

We do not need to take our anger out on other
people. This is not being loving toward them. And we
do not need to carry our anger long. Anger is a
heavy load.

Anger is a part of life. As Christians we are
challenged to use it correctly.

 Anger is a powerful emotion, Father. Help me to
control it, rather than let it control me.

List ways you can better handle your anger.

■ GOD WORKS FOR THE GOOD

Rom. 8:28-35:   "And know that in all things God works for the good of those who love him, who have been called according to his purpose" (v. 28).

A young woman walked dejectedly home from work after being passed up for a promotion. A 50-year-old man was told one more time that he was "too old for the job." Out of the hospital door walked the parents of a young boy with cancer. Another family received a phone call that their grandfather had died suddenly.

There are many tragedies in life that drive us to our knees and force us to question God's control of the world. We almost laugh at Paul's statement that in everything God works for the good.

This verse is a statement of faith. Our God is great enough to bring good out of evil. God brings us closer to him in situations that could drive us farther away.

Paul was able to write this statement after looking back on his life—on the beatings, the shipwrecks, the hunger, and the pain.

We can proclaim the truth of this verse because God has taken the greatest evil and brought forth the greatest good. From the death of his Son, God has brought forth salvation for all of humankind. God does work all things for good!

 Father, how great you are! May you help me see you working in the trials of my life.

Remember an incident when God moved in your life to bring good out of evil.

■ PRAYER IS A LOCAL CALL

1 Thess. 5:12-22:   "Pray continually" (v. 17).

It was fun for the Fishers to live in their home town. They both had a good relationship with their parents. Though their parents lived on the far side of town, they were no farther away than a phone call. Both of the Fishers would find themselves at least once a day picking up the phone and calling their parents—just to talk.

Then Mr. Fisher received a promotion and a transfer. The Fishers moved to another part of the state. Now it was a long-distance call to one of their parents. Though they were tempted to call their parents many times, they limited themselves to once or twice a month.

In our prayer lives we often treat prayer as a long-distance call. We feel a need to have a certain amount of undisturbed time for prayer. We don't pray often, and only at a specific time of day. When we do pray, we load a whole day's thoughts and concerns into it. Sometimes we forget something.

Prayer for a Christian is a local call. When we realize this, we begin to follow the direction of Paul and pray continually. The lines are always open. When something good happens, we can immediately give thanks to God. When trouble occurs, we can pray for help.

Prayer is not a time of day, but a part of life itself.

 Help me, Lord, to keep in constant communication with you.

Practice praying immediately when a prayer need arises.

■ FULL CONCENTRATION

Luke 9:57-62: "No one who puts his hand to the plow and looks back is fit for service in the kingdom of God" (v. 62).

The job seemed simple enough, thought Jim, even if it was a bit boring. He was hired by a farmer to plow one of his fields. He had no doubt he could do the job.

Jim started his job with determination, but soon boredom set in. A flock of geese flying north for the summer caught his attention, and so did cattle in the next field. He daydreamed about the end of school and a summer of fun. When he saw his work, he was dismayed. His rows curved; he even missed parts of the field. It was a bad job.

Christians often find themselves in a position like Jim's. We have been called to a disciplined life, a life that takes our full concentration. But some parts of a Christian's life are not exciting. At times studying the Bible gets dull and praying seems a chore. Serving others turns into a major effort, and it's even hard to get up for church on Sundays.

We begin to wander toward the things that seem more exciting, things that distract us from our service of God and draw us farther from him.

Our hand has been put to the plow. Jesus challenges us to keep our attention on him.

 Lord Jesus, forgive me when my attention wanders from you.

Give up an activity in your life that distracts you from serving God.